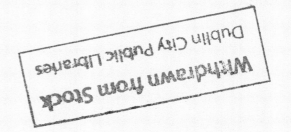
And for mains...

Recipes, stories and pints with an Irish butcher and a chef

Gaz Smith and Rick Higgins

NINE BEAN ROWS

Contents.

Gaz and Rick	1
The book	15
A few notes	16
Shellfish	19
Seafood	43
The perfect storm: The story of Dublin crab	61
Meat	77
Rick's butchery masterclass	115
Steaks and reverse searing	125
From farm to fork: The journey from the field to your plate	141
One-pot wonders	157
Sandwiches and burgers	169
Salads and sides	181
A Dublin pub crawl	205
The morning after: Battle of the breakfasts	216
Sauces and butters	223
Desserts	249
The Higgins' crew	259
The Michael's crew	263
Index	268
Acknowledgements	271

Gaz and Rick.

Gaz Smith

I've always been obsessed with food.

Whether it's an epic multicourse dinner knocked out by one of Irelands's top chefs or a greasy snack box eaten at midnight, I love it all.

That said, I fell into cooking. All this started as a bit of a happy accident. I got my first kitchen job when I was 16. At the time I had moved out of the house and was living in Oxford, so I got the job purely to pay the rent. I wasn't the best student in school, really – I missed most of my exams and was working full time when I was 14.

Turns out I loved it. I quickly went from a kitchen porter to a cook and I thought I was the mutt's nuts. I was always getting myself into mischief and trouble, but I always had a good work ethic.

Then I moved to Ireland, got a job in a proper kitchen and realised I actually couldn't cook at all. So I started from scratch and decided to learn properly. I'd pore over cookbooks every night, absorbing every little detail and building up my ideas. I was obsessed with the idea of creating recipes.

I worked in some brilliant places over the years, from Chapter One to the Chart House, 1014 and Kinara. Then, just as the recession hit in 2008 and was starting to take hold in Ireland, my wife Rita and I had a chance to go to Vienna. She supported the choice to move, just like she has supported me for the 20 years that we've been together.

We fell in love with the city straight away. The people in Vienna love the Irish. The minute you say you're from Ireland, their hearts just melt. It was in Vienna where I really came into my own as a chef.

But my German was awful. Plus I knew that if I stayed there, I'd always be working for someone else. It was my dream to have my own place and work for myself. I didn't have a penny, but I knew that if I could get back home to Ireland, onto my own turf, I could make the moves that I knew I had in me. Taking over the restaurant Michael's was just the ticket.

I started Michael's with zero capital and it took real force to get it over the line because everybody said no – the bank wouldn't give us a loan and the suppliers wouldn't give us credit terms, so we had to be proactive. We jumped in the car and started to go to the producers directly, basically begging to get their produce with the promise of paying on time.

One day, we sat down with Maria Flynn from Ballymakenny Farm. I don't think she knows how important that day was to us. We knew nobody, but she made us tea and a bowl of spuds and we left that day as firm friends. Then we got on board with Steven Farren, Ger and Rob Markey and quickly got sorted with the most incredible crab and lobster. That's really what set us apart.

We had so much support from the start. The people of Mount Merrion saw the effort that we put in and appreciated us for it. We had some lovely support from the media and to my genuine surprise we won some awards. I felt like a fraud accepting them, if I'm honest. It was pure imposter syndrome – all we were doing was cooking a bit of fish in garlic and lemon butter. In fact, that's still what we're doing to this day. But you know what? It works!

Meeting Rick was another big turning point in our story. I remember when I first put in my order, he was like, 'And how are you going to pay for all this?' I left my credit card behind the till and told him to charge me every week. It took me a drunken coin toss a year later to finally get him to agree to a 30-day credit term, but we really bonded.

The key is trust. We both take it all seriously. Sure, we bicker and take the piss out of each other constantly. But during the first lockdowns in 2020, we really held each other up and emerged from them stronger and wiser.

He's a bollix, but his meat is good.

He's a bollix, but his meat is good.

Gaz Smith

Rick Higgins

I am a fourth-generation butcher, born and raised in Baldoyle, North Dublin. My dad, Tony Higgins, is my hero, so I wanted to be just like him. I went to college, but after a month I realised that it wasn't really for me. I knew that my true passion lay in becoming a butcher, just like my father.

Some of my earliest memories are in a butcher shop. I remember when I was seven years old being brought into my Uncle Tom's butcher shop in Sutton Cross, which my dad ran. We helped clear out the fridges and got the place ready for the onslaught of work that lay ahead for them in the Christmas rush.

I was 10 years old when my dad opened his first shop in Portmarnock and my mam, Rose, worked there too. Myself and my two sisters were brought in every Saturday to help out in the shop – I think it also served as a babysitting service so they could keep an eye on us. I instantly fell in love with it, while my two sisters despised it. This is the place where I would serve my time as an apprentice.

I was really lucky that my dad was an old-school butcher, breaking and boning beef himself. The training I had was second to none – others could only dream of it. I fell in love with being a butcher really quickly and I picked up my work ethic from both my mam and my dad. I used to go into work on a Sunday when the shop was closed to prep for the week ahead, practising all the skills that my dad had taught me that particular week.

And then there's my wife, Eva. I'm so lucky with Eva. She understands my drive and passion and backs me 100%. She is definitely my rock, my best friend and I love her to bits. She puts up with all my shit – working late, working Sundays and going for 'business meetings' (AKA pints) with Gaz.

When I started Higgins Family Butcher back in 2013, I had a clear vision: to be the best butcher in the country. I wanted to have an old-school ethos while bringing my own twist to it, carefully sourcing and ageing only the absolute best meats. That plan has never deviated since day one.

I'm a meat fan, plain and simple. For me, there's a huge sense of accomplishment from the journey, from seeing the cow in the field to the moment it arrives in my ageing rooms, then the glorious smell when you cut into the perfect steak and the customer telling me how much they enjoyed it.

Soon, my strict criteria started to get noticed by chefs across the country. I had heard of Gaz and Michael's but knew very little about him until one day he and Rita rocked up to the shop. He introduced himself and began to tell me a little bit about his background. I like to think I'm a pretty good judge of character and I thought to myself I could probably work with this guy. He didn't seem to have an ego — he seemed like a normal bloke who I could relate to.

Now, he'll probably tell you about how I set out my payment terms immediately and it's true, I did. But when he gave me his card details and told me to take payment on my terms, it set my mind at ease. I was warned never to go for a pint with him or I would need a couple days off afterwards. The first time I agreed to go for one or two pints with him in the Sheds in Clontarf, I learned exactly what people meant.

I fell out of the place.

But while having them pints, I realised this bloke is just like me. He loves good food and loves what he does. But he also loves the craic, a pint and a takeaway. The more we worked together and bounced off each other, the more we became mates.

I think he pushes me along, coming up with all sorts of crazy ideas that set off the light bulbs in my brain. Then that turns the idea into something awesome. Sometimes it works, sometimes it doesn't, but both of us push the boundaries and spur each other on. It always starts from a random text: 'Any curveballs? Cow's lips? Sheep's balls?' I love it — it's almost like a test for me to see if I can source something that most people would consider too much hassle.

I think the fact that both of us are perfectionists when it comes to our careers is why we work so well together. Our process is simple. Normally I get a random text from him that just reads: 'Pint?' Then I convince Eva that I'm going to meet Gaz to talk about the plan for the next week. After about six or seven pints we come up with something that's a little off the wall. Then we flip a coin for that week's prices. His face when I win is priceless and I always have a little 10-minute sulk when I lose.

I choose the beef from Castledermot by video call each week. Then I'll get a call from Gaz asking if he can drop out so we can select beef for the week. He'll inevitably rock in all cheery when I'm up to my eyes, but in fairness, the process works. It's easy for me to work with a chef who's as into what I do as I am.

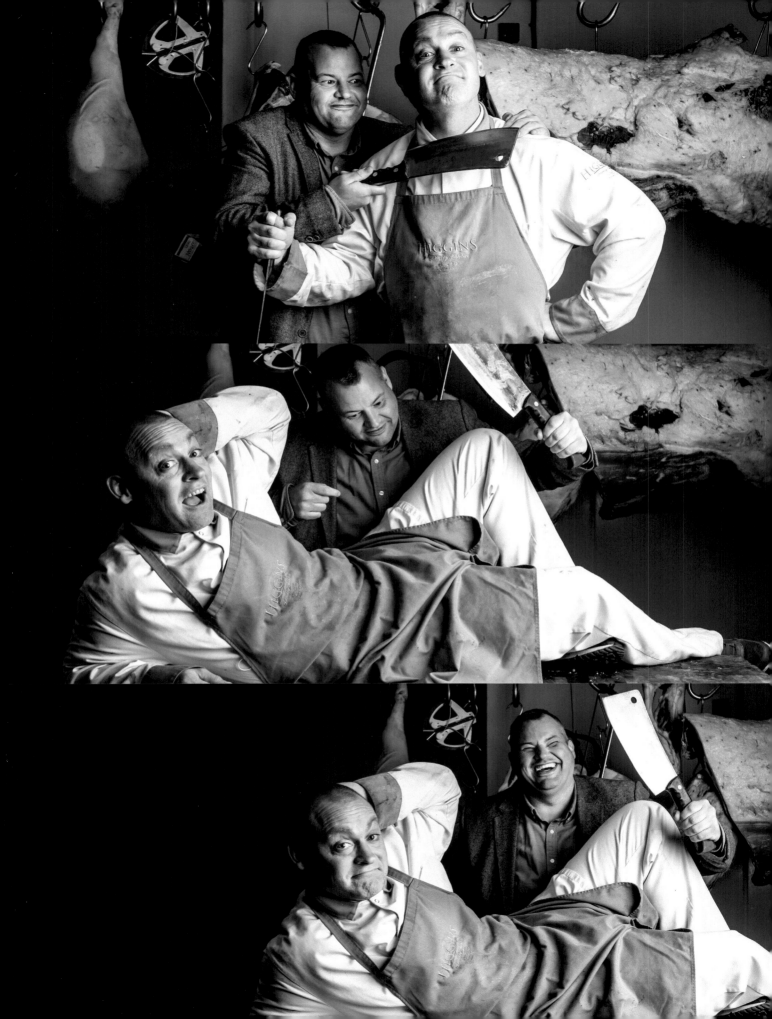

But while having them pints, I realised this bloke is just like me. He loves good food and loves what he does. But he also loves the craic, a pint and a takeaway.

The more we worked together and bounced off each other, the more we became mates. I think he pushes me along, coming up with all sorts of crazy ideas that set off the light bulbs in my brain. Then that turns the idea into something awesome.

Rick Higgins

The book.

I've always wanted to write a book. Even when I was in school and hated studying, I loved to write stories. But Rick and I weren't in a hurry to do this until we found the right people. We wanted to make the book that we wanted to write and tell the story that we wanted to tell.

This book is filled with the kind of things that I love to make. It's not about wanky recipes that require loads of expensive bits of kit and special skills. It's about the kind of cooking that I do at home, which is why there are so many dishes that are made with really forgiving cuts of meat that you can put in an oven and leave for hours (while you nip off for a few pints). We've got the dishes you'll know and love from Michael's but also a few curveballs in there so that you can get creative.

But this is more than just a recipe book.

It's about the people who make what we do special – the producers, farmers and fishermen who work their arses off to bring us the most incredible ingredients to cook with. We also brought in Barry Stephens, of Dublin's 147 Deli, to share some of his banging recipes. This book is about the story behind the food and the people behind the dishes.

We wanted to tell our story, in our words. And that's exactly what we've done.

Gaz Smith

A few notes.

Shopping

We wanted our recipes to be made with ingredients that are easy to find. There's nothing more off-putting than a long list of ingredients that you'll struggle to track down. You should be able to find everything here in a supermarket as well as a good Eastern European and Asian shop. There are even recipes here made using ingredients you could find in a petrol station.

Butter

It should go without saying, but when a recipe includes butter, that means salted butter. Proper, salted butter. And don't even get me started on margarine, it has no place on the planet, let alone in a kitchen.

Seasoning and herbs

In most of my recipes, you'll see me refer to a 'pinch' of something. Now, this isn't a stingy little pinch between your thumb and forefinger. This is a good chef's pinch, using all your fingers and your thumb.

When a 'pinch' refers to herbs, this means a big pinch of the herbs on their stalks. Imagine a good clump of thyme or parsley, before you remove the leaves.

I use flat-leaf parsley unless stated otherwise. That's because it's a little more delicate on a dish that doesn't include much cooking time. If I'm making a stew or something slow cooked, I use curly parsley.

Ovens and cooking times

Just like people, all ovens are made a little different. We have tested our recipes in professional and home ovens, but no one knows the quirks of your own oven like you do. One thing that makes life easier is a digital meat probe thermometer, the kind with a long cable, but you can also just use your own instincts. If you think something requires a little more time in the oven, go for it.

Maggi Liquid Seasoning

I hummed and hawed for ages about whether or not to include this. When you go to London, you see a little bottle of it on all the tables in the coolest, edgiest restaurants. Everyone uses it – it's like super condensed soy sauce and is a flavour bomb of umami. The only downside is that it's packed with MSG. Whether or not you want to use it is completely up to you, but it's what I use at home and I couldn't bring myself to lie to you.

Stock cubes and jarred sauces

I'm not a precious chef (no shit, says you). When it comes to stocks and sauces, I'd much rather you use a stock cube than not make a recipe at all. I love making a slow-cooked tomato sauce like our New York-style 'gravy' (page 228), but I always have a few jars of Dolmio knocking around in the kitchen. Use what you have and don't worry about the food snobs telling you to make everything from scratch.

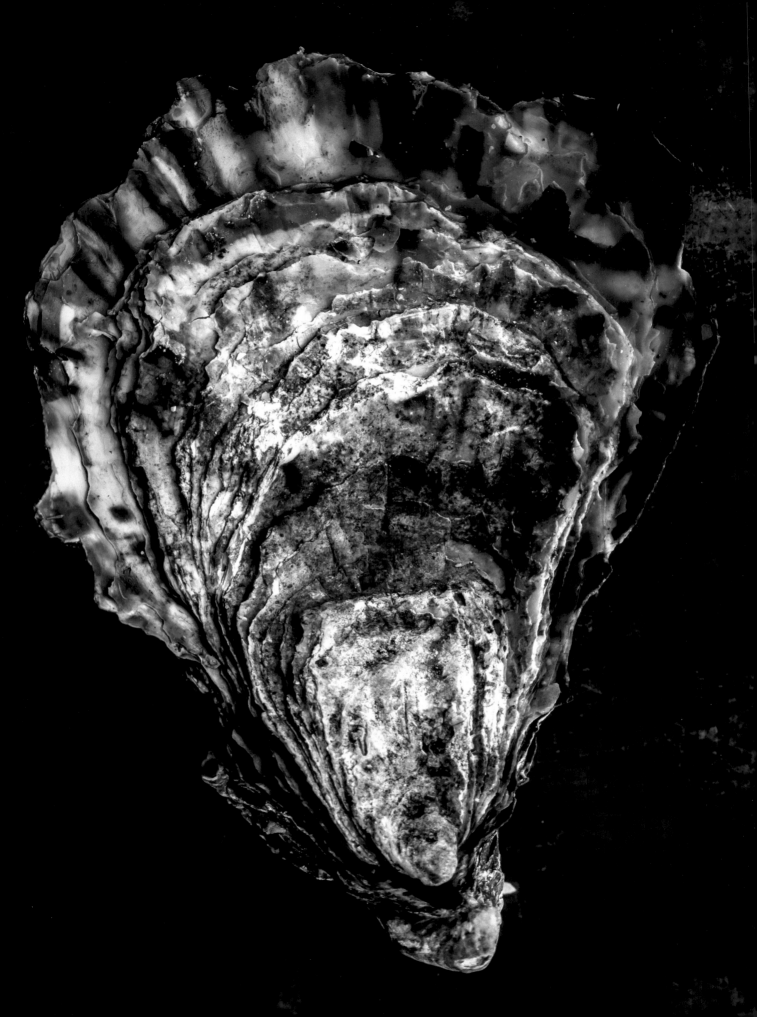

Shellfish.

Oysters with a Bloody Mary sauce   23

Oysters with a hazelnut and tarragon vinaigrette   24

Mussels in a coconut, chilli and coriander seed broth   27

Seared scallops with cucumber and mint gazpacho   29

Crab claws in garlic and lemon butter   30

Grilled prawns in a caramel and fish sauce glaze   32

Dublin Bay prawns   34

Crab salad with avocado purée and pickled cucumber   37

Crab omelette   39

Cockle linguine   40

Oysters with a Bloody Mary sauce

You know the kind of hangover that just screams out for a Bloody Mary? When you're not exactly bedridden and dry heaving but you're definitely not running on all cylinders either? This is exactly the dish you need. It's effectively 'kill or cure' but with more panache. Plus, as there's a whole lot going on flavour wise, it's also the perfect way to serve oysters to people who claim they don't like them.

The dressing has a real feisty kick to it from both the vodka and the Tabasco. You take the oyster like a shot, but don't just send it straight down the hatch – you want to let all these flavours have a little party in your mouth. Then you'll be back in fighting form in no time.

Serves 4

12 oysters, shucked, detached and put back in the half shell

For the Bloody Mary sauce
250ml tomato juice (we love Granini)
100ml vodka
3 tablespoons lemon juice
2 tablespoons good-quality passata
2 tablespoons Tabasco sauce
2 tablespoons Worcestershire sauce
A pinch of celery salt
A good crack of freshly ground black pepper

Put all the sauce ingredients in a mixing bowl and whisk to combine.

Drizzle a generous tablespoon of the Bloody Mary sauce on top of each oyster right before serving. You should have enough sauce left over for a sneaky shot on the side – chef's treat!

Slurp 'em down and feel the horrors melt right out of you.

Oysters with a hazelnut and tarragon vinaigrette

Gaz says

If you ask me, nothing beats a nice, fat, juicy oyster. A good oyster will always be good, whether you eat it with a dash of Tabasco or just slurp it down naked as the day it was shucked. But if you want to do something a little bit special, this is a banging dish to try.

Like so much in life, when you're picking your oyster, you want a big fat wet one. If they look dry from the outside, they're going to be dry on the inside, so go for a shell that has a bit of a glisten to it. Oysters should feel heavier than they look and they should be full to the brim with juices too.

The key to this dish is getting a very good vinegar and being really generous with the tarragon leaves – if I'm eating tarragon, I want to know about it. The slight sweetness of the tarragon marries perfectly with the sharpness of the vinegar and the hazelnuts bring an earthy sweetness to the whole affair. That, matched with the fat, slippery, salty oysters, makes the whole dish a match made in heaven.

Serves 4

12 fresh oysters, shucked, detached and put back in the half shell

For the dressing
20g skinned and roasted hazelnuts, very finely chopped
1 banana shallot, very finely diced
28 fresh tarragon leaves, very finely sliced
8 tablespoons white wine vinegar
A good crack of freshly ground black pepper

Put all the dressing ingredients in a mixing bowl and whisk to combine.

Serve the oysters in their shells with roughly ½ teaspoon of the vinaigrette spooned right on top of the flesh. I'm talking about the oyster flesh, you absolute dirt bird.

Mussels in a coconut, chilli and coriander seed broth

600g wild mussels, cleaned, debearded and well rinsed
2 tablespoons sunflower oil
1 medium white onion, finely diced
2 garlic cloves, finely diced
1 x thumb-sized piece of ginger, peeled and grated or finely diced
1 small fresh red chilli, thinly sliced (see the chef's tip)
1 tablespoon red curry paste
A pinch of coriander seeds
Zest and juice of 2 limes
Zest and juice of ½ orange
1 x 400ml tin of coconut milk
100ml pouring cream
1 tablespoon Maggi Liquid Seasoning or fish sauce
2 big pinches of finely chopped fresh flat-leaf parsley and coriander

To serve
Crusty bread

First off, be sure to wash the mussels really well and before you cook them, check that they're all firmly closed or that they close up when you tap them. If you're in any doubt, chuck it. It's not worth the risk.

Get the biggest saucepan that you have (you know, the annoying one that you keep on top of the kitchen cupboards) and heat the oil in it over a medium heat. Add the onion and sauté for 3–4 minutes before adding the garlic and cooking for a further 2–3 minutes.

Add the ginger, red chilli, curry paste, coriander seeds and the citrus zest and juice and combine well. Keep the paste moving around the pan and spread it as thinly as you can without it sticking. This will help to release all the beautiful oils and aromas. Cook out for another 4–5 minutes before adding the coconut milk, cream and Maggi Liquid Seasoning or fish sauce. Simmer gently for 5–6 minutes.

Give the mussels another quick rinse and check for any open ones one more time before putting them all into the sauce. Ideally, your mussels are never more than three deep in the pan. Pop a lid on and cook over a high heat for 3 minutes. Keep the pan moving.

After 3 minutes, remove the lid and check that they are starting to open before giving them a good stir. Continue to cook for a further 2 minutes with the lid on. By this stage, all the mussels should be open. If any of them remain closed, chuck them in the bin.

Throw in the herbs right at the end and ladle into bowls with fresh crusty bread on the side.

Gaz says
I think there should be eating and drinking in a good bowl of mussels. In my house, we all eat them in a different way. I sit and shell all of mine, then plop them in the sauce and eat them all in one go, like a mussel chowder. My son Felix eats them one by one, using the shell as a little pincer. My daughter Gabi eats them all in their shells. Rita is a bit odd, and not just because she married me. She'll shell five at a time, eat those, then shell the next five.

Chef's tip
When it comes to chillies, one day you could put four chillies into something and not taste them at all and the next day you could put in half a chilli and get absolutely hoofed out of it. So always take a tiny taste of your fresh chillies to see how hot (or not) they are and use them accordingly. Or if you fancy a surprise, roll the dice and see what you get.

Serves 2–3

Seared scallops with cucumber and mint gazpacho

12 large, plump, fresh scallops (see the chef's tip)
2 teaspoons sunflower oil

For the gazpacho
1 large cucumber, peeled and deseeded
1 garlic clove, finely chopped
20 fresh coriander leaves
10 fresh mint leaves
Zest and juice of 1 lime (save the zest for the garnish)
150ml buttermilk
2 tablespoons Greek yoghurt
½ tablespoon horseradish sauce
1 teaspoon coriander seeds
4 large pinches of fine sea salt
2 good cracks of freshly ground black pepper
1 teaspoon honey (optional)

To garnish
1 small bunch of fresh dill, leaves snipped

Chop the cucumber into rough chunks, then throw them into a food processor or blender along with all the other gazpacho ingredients. Blitz it up until it's nice and smooth. Have a taste to see if it needs any honey – sometimes cucumbers can be a little salty or bland and a teaspoon of honey can jazz them up nicely.

Dry the scallops really well with kitchen paper, but don't season them before cooking as it will draw out more moisture.

Heat 1 teaspoon of the oil in a non-stick frying pan over a very high heat. When the oil is smoking, carefully add the first six scallops one by one, flat side down. Here's a handy trick: start by putting the first one at the 12 o'clock position, then put the others around the pan in a clockwise manner, roughly 10 seconds apart. That way, you can be sure they've all cooked for the same amount of time by flipping them over and removing them from the pan in the correct order.

Cook each scallop for 2–3 minutes, until the bottom is darkly caramelised and well charred. Using tongs, gently lift each scallop up from the heat and turn it over, remembering to work in the same clockwise direction. Continue cooking for a further minute or so. They'll puff up and stand tall when they're perfectly cooked.

Remove from the pan and allow them to rest on kitchen paper. Now is the time to give them a good seasoning with salt and pepper. Repeat with the second batch of six scallops.

Serve three scallops per person in a chilled bowl of gazpacho, sprinkled with lime zest and snipped dill leaves.

Gaz says
As you know, gazpacho is usually made with tomatoes. But this cucumber version is really fresh and fragrant, with some zing from the lime, aroma from the mint and a bit of a sour kick from the buttermilk. When you add a beautifully seared, slightly sweet scallop into the mix, it all just works so well. Plus you can have it all done and on the plate in 15 minutes.

I love to caramelise scallops. To me, they should nearly be burnt. What you want is a nice charred exterior and an almost raw interior – I call it 'black and blue'. Don't be afraid to really sear the hell out of them, as they're quite hardy little buggers. Just don't overcook them or they'll taste like little rubber bouncy balls.

Chef's tip
The cooking times in this recipe are based on large scallops (roughly 85g). If yours are smaller, adjust the cooking time and check them after 1 minute. If you can't get scallops, this dish works really well with prawns. Just sear them in the pan as you would the scallops.

**Serves 2 as a main
or 4 as a starter**

Crab claws in garlic and lemon butter

Gaz says

There's no way I could write this book without writing about crab claws. I'm not exaggerating when I say that this is the dish that put Michael's on the map. Without this crab, we wouldn't be where we are today. But that's not (just) due to my impeccable talent, intelligence and skill. It's all down to the crab that we source from the lads in Lambay Island, which you can read about on pages 61–75.

There's not much technical skill to this dish, but it rises and falls on the quality of the crab. If you can't get decent claws, don't bother making it at all – it would only disappoint. It's just not the same with frozen or sub-par claws.

I prefer to use smaller claws, as they are packed with flavour. I think of it as warming up the crab rather than cooking it – you don't want to serve it piping hot.

Serves 1

6 coriander seeds
3 garlic cloves, finely chopped
60g butter
200g cooked and deshelled crab claws
2 pinches of fine sea salt
A pinch each of finely chopped fresh coriander, dill and flat-leaf parsley
Zest and juice of 1 lemon

To serve
Crusty bread

Warm the coriander seeds in a dry frying pan over a medium heat and very lightly toast until all those delicious aromas are released.

Add the chopped garlic to the same pan along with the butter and crab claws. Once the butter has melted, turn down the heat to its lowest setting.

Add two pinches of salt and toss it all gently in the pan for a maximum of 4 minutes. Remember, the crab is already cooked – you're just warming it through. Crab is best served warm, not hot, so don't go overboard with the cooking.

Right at the end, add the chopped herbs and the lemon zest and juice.

You'll want to eat this with some crusty white bread for mopping up all that sexy, sexy sauce. Pair it with a glass of really cold white wine and you'll be in a state of food bliss.

Grilled prawns in a caramel and fish sauce glaze

Gaz says

One of my favourite things to do is fuck off to London on a jolly – sorry, a very important 'food research trip' – and eat as much as humanly possible in the space of a few days. I'll visit six or seven restaurants, eat and drink the whole menu and roll myself home at the end. But my first port of call is always the same: the Smoking Goat in Shoreditch. It's loud, it's raucous, it's spicy and you'll always eat something there that you've never had before. But you always start off with the fish sauce-glazed chicken wings and two cold beers as you sit at the bar and wait for your table. For my money, it's the best eight quid you can spend anywhere in London.

This recipe isn't a rip-off, but rather a nod to that classic dish. To me, the pairing of fish sauce with a spicy syrup is just genius. It's one distinct flavour blended with another and both lift the other one up. We do it with prawns, which really hold up to the sticky, spicy, crack-like glaze.

Once you've tasted this, it'll stay on your lips for a month.

Chef's tip

If you're pushed for time, you can simply add the prawns straight into the hot syrup and cook them in there.

Serves 2

Sunflower oil
12 big fat prawns, deshelled and deveined

For the caramel and fish sauce glaze
100g caster sugar
80ml lime juice (roughly the juice of 3 plump, ripe limes)
4 garlic cloves, finely chopped
1 x 5cm chunk of fresh ginger, peeled and grated
Zest of 2 limes
5 tablespoons Kikkoman soy sauce
1 tablespoon fish sauce
1 teaspoon chilli flakes

Put all the glaze ingredients in a frying pan on a medium heat. Bring everything to a simmer until the sugar has melted and it starts to reduce into a syrup. Lower the heat slightly and reduce down for 3–4 minutes.

Get another frying pan on a high heat with a splash of oil. Add the prawns to the spanking hot pan and sear for 2–3 minutes. When they're done, slather them all in the glaze – but only put the glaze in the pan for the last 30 seconds because otherwise it'll burn, baby, burn.

Serve immediately.

Dublin Bay prawns

Gaz says

To me, there's nothing quite like Dublin Bay prawns. Give me prawns over lobster any day of the week. When they're good, they're just so, so good. And they don't need any messing around with either. All you need is a hot pan, salt and lemon. That's it.

A good fresh prawn should be slightly feathery, never firm and rubbery, and it should take some teasing to get out of the shell. This is my favourite way to eat – sat in the garden with a few really good Dublin Bay prawns in front of me and a cold beer in my hand. It's almost meditative, sitting there and rooting around in the shells, sucking out the brains. It's eating as it should be – primal, simple and fucking delicious.

Chef's tip

Dublin Bay prawns can be very expensive. My advice is to buy the largest you can and have four huge ones instead of six or seven smaller ones.

Serves 2

Sunflower oil
16 whole Dublin Bay prawns, shell on (roughly 60g each)
16 garlic cloves, roughly chopped
2 lemons, halved widthways
2 teaspoons butter (use the garlic and lemon butter on page 244 if you like)
A handful of fresh flat-leaf parsley, finely chopped
Extra virgin olive oil
Fine sea salt and freshly ground black pepper

Put a splash of sunflower oil in a large frying pan on a high heat and heat until it's smoking. Add the whole prawns to the pan. After 1 minute, turn the prawns and cook them on the other side for a further minute. At this stage, you should be getting a whopper aroma off of the prawn shells. Don't worry if they start to blacken – the shells are protecting the meat inside like the precious cargo that it is.

Add the garlic and halved lemons to the pan. Season with black pepper and dollop the butter into the pan. Cover with a lid, turn off the heat and leave for about 90 seconds or so.

Serve the prawns with chopped fresh parsley and a drizzle of extra virgin olive oil. Pop a small bowl of salt on the table too – when you take the prawn out of the shell, give him a little sprinkle before you eat.

Crab salad with avocado purée and pickled cucumber

For the crab mayo
2 heaped tablespoons mayonnaise
2 garlic cloves, finely chopped
Zest of 2 lemons, juice of 1
Zest of 1 orange, juice of ½
A handful of fresh coriander, chopped
A pinch of fine sea salt
400g fresh white crab meat

For the pickled cucumber
75g caster sugar
90ml white wine vinegar
1 x 2cm round thin slice of fresh ginger
A good pinch of fine sea salt
1 cucumber, skin on and sliced into 2mm-thick rounds

For the avocado purée
200g avocado, peeled and stoned (roughly 1 large avocado)
Juice of 1 large lemon
1 teaspoon mayonnaise
1 teaspoon icing sugar
1 teaspoon fine sea salt

To serve
Snipped fresh dill
A good crack of freshly ground black pepper
Lemon wedges
Crusty bread

Gaz says
This dish has been on the Michael's menu since day one. In fact, I first started making something similar when I was 15, working under a classically trained French head chef. There's something about crab and avocado that just works. It's one of those timeless combinations that is a classic for a reason.

Obviously, getting good crab is absolutely crucial. And I hate to break it to you, but you probably won't get the big chunks of crab meat that you'll find in Michael's. Most commercial places take the meat off mechanically, whereas ours is hand-picked and cracked. But it is possible to get the good stuff, even in some supermarkets. Just go for the best that you can afford, but if it's a chalky brown colour, leave it on the shelf where it belongs.

These pickled cucumbers are little flavour bombs and give the whole dish a bit of an edge. I never get bored of them. I've always got a jar of the marinade knocking around, ready to make up a batch whenever I want to spruce up a sandwich or just eat it with some cheese and crackers.

Chef's tip
You can make the marinade in advance, but don't pour it over the sliced cucumbers until you're almost ready to eat. Cucumbers are more delicate than gherkins and will release water into the marinade and dilute it if they're left to their own devices for too long.

Serves 4

To make the pickled cucumber, add the sugar, vinegar, ginger and salt to a small saucepan and bring to a gentle boil. Swirl the syrup in the pan to check that all the sugar has dissolved, then remove from the heat and leave it to cool.

Pop the cucumber slices into a medium-sized mixing bowl. Once the pickling liquid is cool, pour it over the cucumber rounds and allow them to soak in the syrup for 15 minutes.

To make the avocado purée, add all the ingredients to a food processor and blitz until smooth.

Now, on to the crab mayo! Combine the mayo and garlic in a medium-sized bowl and give it a good mix before adding the citrus zest and juice. Mix it all well, then add the chopped coriander. Season to taste with some salt, then add the crab and combine it very gently to ensure the meat is coated evenly.

To assemble, place about 10 slices of pickled cucumber onto the plate, pop a good tablespoon of the avocado purée on top, then finish with the dressed crab. Garnish with a bit of fresh dill and a crack of black pepper and serve with a lemon wedge and slices of toasted crusty bread.

Crab omelette

4 eggs
2 big knobs of butter, softened
2 big handfuls of baby spinach, finely chopped
A few cherry tomatoes, chopped (only if you have really nice ones to hand)
2 pinches of grated Cheddar cheese
A pinch of finely chopped fresh dill
A pinch of finely chopped fresh flat-leaf parsley
2 tablespoons milk (or cream if you have it knocking around)
1 tablespoon vegetable oil
100g fresh white crab meat
A lemon wedge
Fine sea salt and freshly ground black pepper

Break the eggs into a large bowl and run a fork through gently to break them up. Don't use a whisk or overbeat the mixture. You want a bit of texture in there.

Add one knob of softened butter and give it another mix, then add the spinach, tomatoes, Cheddar, fresh herbs and milk.

Heat up the oil and the other knob of butter in a 23cm frying pan on a low to medium heat. Just as the butter starts to colour, add the egg mix. Using a spatula, pull the omelette in from the sides of the pan at the quarter marks, like you're making the sign of the cross. Leave it alone for 2 minutes, when it should just be starting to set.

Pop in half of the crab meat on top of the egg, then either put the pan under a preheated grill or put a lid on the pan and cook until the omelette is slightly set. Personally, I like a runny omelette so I don't fully cook it. But you do you.

Turn it out onto a plate and scatter the remaining crab on top. Finish it off with a squeeze of lemon and a generous dousing of salt and pepper, bearing in mind the mix hasn't been seasoned.

Put the telly on, hide your phone under a sofa cushion and eat while watching *Game of Thrones*.

Gaz says
In case you hadn't noticed by now, I quite like crab. And this is a really simple way to eat it that feels special but requires next to no effort at all. This is the perfect thing to make when you're just in from work and want to whip something up quickly that you can eat in front of the telly while still feeling a bit like Little Lord Fauntleroy.

Chef's tip
The key to making a good omelette is seasoning it at the end, right before you're about to eat. If you season raw egg, it makes the mixture split.

Serves 1

Cockle linguine

Gaz says

Did you ever watch the movie *Chef*? If you have, you'll remember the pasta recipe that's basically the main character. It's so simple, but it leaves everyone (including Scarlett Johansson) weak at the knees. This is my version of that. And I look forward to the day I cook it for Scarlett.

When I first started training as a chef, I used to think that a pasta dish had to have a million ingredients in it to be good. You remember those days – everything had pine nuts, spinach, chorizo, chilli. But as I matured as a chef (not as a person, don't worry), I realised it's the pasta that should sing. The sauce should just give it a little nudge towards Flavourtown.

This dish is a piece of piss to make. The cockles will cook in 90 seconds and if you're using fresh pasta, that'll only take a few minutes to cook too. Basically, you can walk in the front door and have the whole lot on a plate in front of you in less time than it takes to order a pizza.

Chef's tip

When you cook pasta, make sure your cooking water is as salty as the sea – in fact, you want it to be *too* salty. There's nothing worse than pasta that's been cooked in unsalted water. And make sure you slightly undercook the pasta too so that it'll slurp up the sauce and absorb all the flavour when you mix the two together.

Serves 2

240g fresh linguini
2 teaspoons fine sea salt
100g butter
440g cockles
6 garlic cloves, minced
3–4 pinches of chilli flakes
50ml white wine
A big pinch of chopped fresh flat-leaf parsley
A squeeze of lemon

Cook the pasta according to the packet instructions, minus 2 minutes. You want the cooking water to be as salty as the sea – use 1 teaspoon of salt for every litre of water. For 240g of linguini you'll want to use 2 litres of water, so that's 2 teaspoons of salt.

While the pasta is cooking, melt the butter in a large frying pan over a medium heat. Add the cockles, garlic and chilli flakes and toss well. Add your glug of white wine and cook off for 3 minutes.

When the pasta has 2 minutes left, use a pair of tongs to lift it up out of the water and straight into the frying pan, making sure you reserve about 3 tablespoons of the cooking water. Toss it all really well, until the pasta has absorbed the sauce. If any of the cockles haven't yet opened fully, discard them.

Add 2–3 tablespoons of the reserved cooking water and mix it all really well in the frying pan for a few more seconds, until you're left with a glossy sauce glistening all over the pasta.

Garnish with the chopped fresh parsley and a squeeze of lemon juice. Serve immediately to someone who looks like Scarlett Johansson and watch them fall in love with you after the very first bite.

Seafood.

Seafood chowder   47

Fish and chips with pea purée   48

Smoked haddock and prawn lasagne   50

Asian-style tuna tartare   52

Hake and mussels in garlic and lemon butter   55

Black sole on the bone with capers and gherkins   56

Barry's Indian-spiced monkfish   58

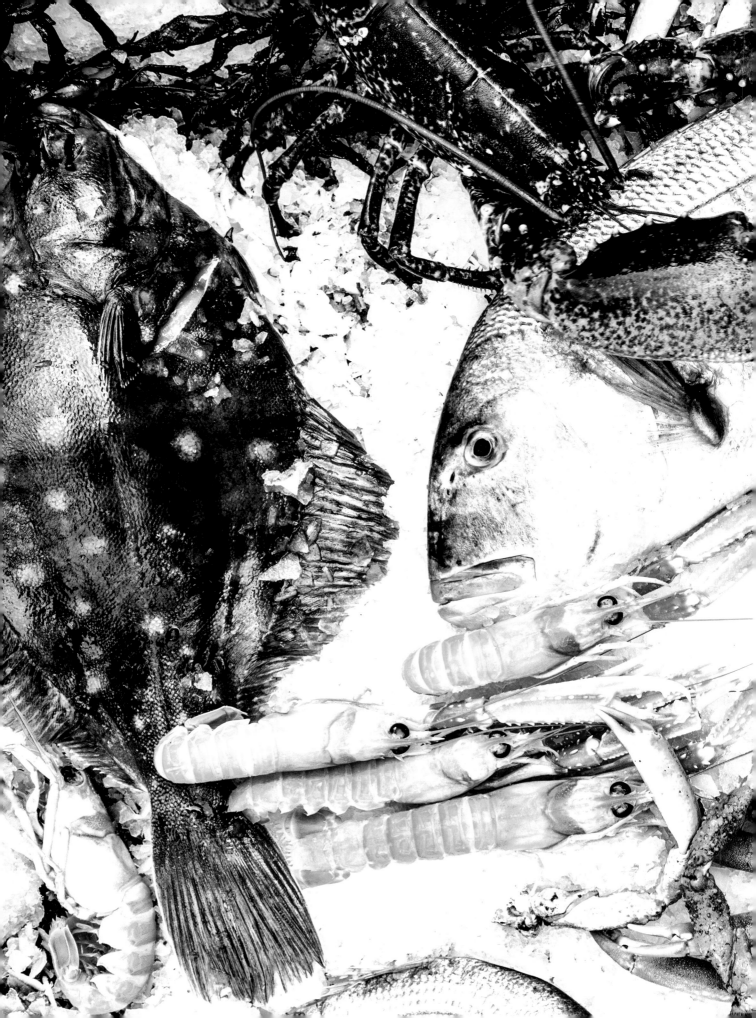

Seafood chowder

Olive oil
1 medium onion, finely diced
100g carrots, peeled and finely diced
100g celery, finely diced
200g potatoes, peeled and cut into 1.5cm cubes
4 garlic cloves, sliced
4 star anise
1 tablespoon coriander seeds
1.2 litres good-quality fish stock (or from a cube is fine)
2 big pinches of fine sea salt
100g leeks, finely diced
150g smoked fish, cubed
100g cockles
100g mussels
100g fresh prawns
80g meaty white fish, diced
200ml pouring cream
Zest and juice of 1 lemon, plus extra juice to finish if you like
A good pinch of finely chopped fresh flat-leaf parsley
A good pinch of finely chopped fresh dill
A good pinch of finely chopped fresh coriander

To serve
Crusty bread

Get a nice big pot and heat a good glug of oil in it over a low heat. Add your onion, carrots, celery, spuds, garlic, star anise and coriander seeds and sauté for 5 minutes, stirring often.

Add your fish stock along with two big pinches of salt and bring to a simmer. Cook for 15 minutes, until the veg are slightly softened and the stock is starting to thicken (you can thank the starch in the potatoes for that). Add your leeks and let the whole lot simmer gently for 15 minutes more.

Raise the temperature to a high heat. Once your base is bubbling, throw in all your seafood and cook for 3 minutes. Turn down the heat to medium, then pour in the cream and cook for a further 2 minutes.

Take your chowder off the heat, add the lemon zest and juice along with all the chopped herbs and stir to combine. You can also finish off each portion with an extra squeeze of lemon if you like.

Serve hot with crusty bread.

Gaz says

If I see chowder on a menu, I almost always go for it. And almost single every time, I'm disappointed. A chowder is one of those things that should be so good, but so many people fuck it up. It's either grey, thick and clumpy or bland and grainy.

The thing is, it's really easy to get it right. Ours is based on a good fish stock – the only thickener comes from the starch in the potatoes. A really good fish stock is amazing, but don't worry if you only have a premade one. I'd rather you make this with a stock cube than not at all. Either way, the key is to chuck the fish in for only the last few minutes. That's how long it takes to cook – if you leave it all sitting in the pot for hours, you've ruined the fish.

Our little curveball comes from coriander seeds and star anise, which works so well. It gives a little bit of a different note and makes the whole dish a smidge more fragrant.

Chef's tip
You can use whatever fish you like, but make sure you use the naturally smoked fish, not that stinky, slimy, orange-dyed gack.

Serves 4 as a starter

Fish and chips with pea purée

Gaz says

We had a right catastrophe during the second lockdown in 2020. We'd decided to turn Little Mike's into a gourmet chipper and people went mad for it. We were using the best turbot, making incredible batter and hand-cutting chips throughout the night. The only problem was that I'd forgotten fish and chips don't travel. At all. After sitting in a wrapped bag for a few minutes, it all turns to shit.

The crisp batter had gone soft. The fish inside may as well have been shitty frozen cod. The beautiful chips were soggy. Letting down my customers, and having to call them one by one to apologise, was one of the hardest moments of lockdown.

But if you're making fish and chips at home, it's simple. The process itself is a quick one too. All your prep has to be done before you put the beer in the batter – you've only got 5 minutes before that batter is dead.

I've got a few tricks up my sleeve. The first is to use the cheapest, fizziest, pissiest beer you can find. This isn't the time for hipster craft ale. The second is my expert batter mixing technique, called Porridge Fingers®. Instead of mixing with a whisk, you mix with your fingers, in a claw shape. If you whisk it you'll get rid of the lumps, but the lumps are what make this batter banging. It should look like porridge, hence the name. Those little lumps burst in the fryer and make those cracking little craggy nooks in the batter, which is exactly what you want. Just promise me you'll eat it straight away.

Serves 2

2 x 200g white fish fillets, skinned (this works well with cod, whiting or haddock, or for something different, skate)
Fine sea salt and freshly ground black pepper
Vegetable oil, for deep-frying
150g plain flour, plus extra for dredging
55g cornflour
1 teaspoon baking powder
250ml ice-cold fizzy beer – only open it the second before you make the batter

For the pea purée
150ml cream
100ml milk
400g frozen peas

To serve
Chips – from the chipper, homecooked or oven chips

To make the pea purée, gently simmer the cream and milk in a saucepan for 1–2 minutes. Add the peas and a generous pinch of salt and simmer for another minute, then transfer to a blender and whizz it all up to form a thick, smooth purée. Set aside.

Pat the fish fillets dry on all sides using kitchen paper, then season the fish really well. Dredge the fillets in flour and dust off the excess. Set these aside while you make the batter to let the flour really fuse onto the fish so that it sticks properly.

Heat the oil to 180°C in a deep-fryer while you make the batter.

In a large bowl, mix together the flour, cornflour, baking powder and 1 teaspoon of salt. Now, and only now, can you open your ice-cold beer, pour it into the bowl and use your Porridge Fingers® to mix together into a rough, lumpy batter.

Now you've got to work quickly! Dip each floured piece into the batter and get a good generous coating on there. Try to only hold it with a finger and a thumb and absolutely drench it in batter. Gently place it into the fat, giving each fillet a little wiggle as you put it in. That way, you get a bit of extra puff in the batter. Don't just chuck it in quickly – show it a bit of tenderness.

As the fish is cooking, feel free to drizzle a little extra batter on it for an additional bit of texture. Fry each fillet for 5–7 minutes, until it's golden brown. Drain on kitchen paper.

Serve immediately with chips and the pea purée.

Smoked haddock and prawn lasagne

Gaz says

I originally had such grand plans for this lasagne. It was going to be packed with lobster cooked down in a bisque made from the shells, but it was soon brought to my attention that not everyone has a blender at home that can pulverise lobster shells. So we changed tack.

This is the perfect thing to make when you want something that's comforting but a little bit different. You're not going to have to tackle a live lobster in your kitchen, but you're still going to create something with a bit of pizazz.

Serves 4

For the béchamel
80g butter
80g plain flour
600ml milk
500ml cream
1 bay leaf
2 pinches of fine sea salt
A good pinch of freshly ground black pepper

For the lasagne
1 tablespoon butter
350g tomato sauce (New York-style 'gravy' on page 228 or shop-bought)
12 lasagne sheets (fresh or non-soak)
300g smoked haddock
300g prawn tails, shelled and deveined
150g grated mozzarella

First things first, make your béchamel. Melt the butter in a large saucepan over a medium heat. Once that's melted, add your flour and cook it out for 3–4 minutes, stirring it with a wooden spoon. You want a nice smooth paste.

Stir in your milk and cream, adding it bit by bit and stirring continuously to avoid lumps.

Once all the milk and cream have been added, chuck the bay leaf in there and season with salt and pepper. Bring the mixture to the boil for 4–5 minutes, until it has thickened up nicely, then remove from the heat and allow it to cool.

Preheat the oven to 190°C.

Now to the fun part. Grease your lasagne dish with the butter. Add a layer of béchamel sauce (aim to use one-quarter of the béchamel here), then a layer of the New York-style 'gravy' or tomato sauce (but use one-third of this sauce). Pop on four lasagne sheets, covering the entire base as best you can.

Pop on another layer of béchamel, then another layer of the tomato sauce (using another quarter of the béchamel and a third of the tomato sauce again), then add half the smoked haddock and prawns, spacing them all out evenly. Lightly season with salt and pepper, then add half the grated mozzarella and top with four more lasagne sheets. You see where we're going with this.

Pop on the third layer of béchamel, then the rest of the tomato sauce. Scatter over the rest of the haddock and prawns and lightly season, then top with the last four lasagne sheets. Now smear the whole lot with a sexy layer of béchamel and the remaining mozzarella.

Pop it into the oven for 20 minutes, then turn the dish around and cook for another 10 minutes. Once cooked, allow to rest for 5 minutes before digging in.

Asian-style tuna tartare

Gaz says

This dish always flies out the door in the restaurant. There's something about it that's so simple but so complex at the same time. You've got all the banging flavours from the Asian dressing and the firm slipperiness of the fresh tuna to boot. The sauce has loads of different background elements, but it still lets the fish sing.

Tell the fishmonger when you're buying the tuna that you're going to be eating it raw and they'll know what to give you. You're looking for tuna that's a deep ruby red with a good bit of fat in it (just make sure you cut the fatty chunks smaller than the flesh). But this also works with plenty of other fish, like salmon or a really fresh mackerel, so feel free to use whatever is freshest at the fishmonger.

Chef's tip

Only combine the dressing and the fish right before serving, otherwise the acid in the dressing will start to cook the fish.

Serves 4 as a starter, 2 as a main or 1 Gaz

125g fresh tuna loin, very finely cubed

For the dressing
50ml Asian dressing (page 234)
2 tablespoons sesame oil
1 tablespoon sweet chilli sauce
Juice of ½ lime
A good pinch of finely chopped fresh coriander

For the avocado cream
2 ripe avocados, peeled and stoned
Juice of 1 lime
1 teaspoon mayonnaise
A good pinch of fine sea salt

To garnish
Black sesame seeds

To serve
8 Thai shrimp crackers, deep-fried (or grab 'em from the local takeaway)

Pour the Asian dressing into a medium-sized bowl and add the sesame oil, sweet chilli sauce, lime juice and coriander. Whisk to combine well and reserve 4 tablespoons for serving in a separate bowl. Set both aside.

To prepare the avocado cream, whizz the avocado flesh, lime juice, mayo and salt in a food processor (or using a stick blender) until you're left with a smooth cream. Make this right before serving, as it'll turn brown if you leave it for longer than a few minutes.

Now add the finely chopped tuna to the bigger bowl of dressing and beat it all together. Don't be afraid to treat it a little rough – you want to break down the tuna ever so slightly.

To serve, smear 1 tablespoon of the avocado cream on a plate and top with the tuna tartare. Pop a couple shrimp crackers on the side and sprinkle the tuna with the black sesame seeds. Have the reserved dressing to hand in case you fancy an extra little drizzle.

Hake and mussels in garlic and lemon butter

4 tablespoons vegetable oil
2 x 200g hake fillets, deboned and skin on
Plain flour, for dusting
Fine sea salt and freshly ground black pepper
200g mussels, debearded, cleaned and well rinsed (see the chef's tip)
½ medium leek, thinly sliced
4 big tablespoons garlic and lemon butter (page 244)
8–9 capers
1 teaspoon Dijon mustard
A big pinch of fresh flat-leaf parsley

To serve
60:40 mash (page 191)
Steamed tenderstem broccoli

Heat up your oil in a non-stick frying pan over a medium heat.

While that's heating up, dry the hake really well with kitchen paper and dip the skin in the tiniest dusting of flour. Give it a good season with salt and pepper.

Add the hake to the pan, skin side down, putting the fish away from you so you don't get splashed with the hot oil. Once the skin has fully touched the pan, don't move it. You want to leave it there, without fiddle arsing around, for 4 minutes. That way, you get a nice crisp skin.

Seriously, I said don't touch it.

If your fish is fresh, you should see it start to turn white on the edges. When the white section is about halfway up the fillet, you can turn it over and cook the other side. Flip it over neatly with a spatula. Again, don't do it too quickly, and once it's in the pan, DON'T TOUCH IT.

Cook the fillets, flesh side down, for 2–3 more minutes. Take them out to rest.

In the same pan, chuck in the mussels, leek and butter, then add the capers, Dijon and parsley into the mix. Give it all a good shake around and pop a lid on. Cook for 2–3 minutes while your hake is resting. Discard any unopened mussels.

Pop it all on a plate, making sure you give your hake a lovely little bath with the buttery juices from the pan.

Serve with 60:40 mash and steamed tenderstem broccoli.

Gaz says
One of the things we're well known for in the restaurants is our platters. They arrive at the table towering with different seafood – today's one had turbot, halibut, monkfish, black sole, mussels, cockles, crab, Dublin Bay prawns and lobster fish cakes, all slathered in lemon butter with golden chips on the side.

We were toying with the idea of putting a seafood platter in the book, but to be honest, it's not something you'd want to make at home. All the fish require different cooking techniques and timings, and if you tried to do this at home without a team of chefs at your disposal, you'd end up in a big sweaty mess, having a secret cry in the corner of the kitchen (again) before kicking the bin and hurting your toe.

So this is our little compromise. You've got a combination of a perfectly cooked piece of fish with some plump little mussels to keep things interesting. You still get a banging meal out of it, but you won't have a nervous breakdown in the kitchen. Leave that nonsense to me.

Chef's tip
Be sure to wash the mussels really well and before you cook them, check that they're all firmly closed or that they close up when you tap them. If you're in any doubt, chuck it. One bad mussel can really fuck up your week.

Serves 2

Black sole on the bone with capers and gherkins

Gaz says

Black sole is one of my favourite kinds of fish, particularly when it's cooked on the bone. It's got that slightly gelatinous, slurpy, lip-smacking texture to it. It's one of the few fish that cooks really well on the bone with no drama. In fact, every time I eat it I feel like I'm in a *Tom and Jerry* cartoon, when the cat eats a whole fish and pulls out the skeleton in one go. It always brings me back to the telly of my childhood.

If you've got the house to yourself for once and you want to have something nice without too much faff, this is a great dish. Sometimes there's nothing better than cooking something good and eating it by yourself with a good book.

Serves 1

1 x 250g black sole, trimmed, skinned and left on the bone
Fine sea salt and freshly ground black pepper
A small glug of vegetable oil
1 tablespoon butter
6–7 capers
4 gherkins, cut into quarters
A pinch of chopped fresh flat-leaf parsley
A pinch of chopped fresh dill

To serve
1 lemon wedge

Pat the fish with kitchen paper to make sure it's fully dry. Season well with salt and pepper.

Pop a frying pan on a medium to high heat until it's just starting to smoke. Add a small glug of oil and reduce the heat to medium.

Place the fish in the pan, moving it away from you so you don't splash yourself with hot oil like an idiot. Once the fish has hit the pan, don't touch it! Leave it where it is for 3–4 minutes, until it's golden brown, then flip it over, add the butter and cook the other side for 3–4 minutes as well. Did I mention not to touch it? Don't touch it.

Turn off the heat, add the capers, gherkins, parsley and dill and let it finish cooking in the residual heat of the pan for 2–3 minutes. If your particular black sole is a bit thick or if you're lucky enough to get a large one, it might need a few minutes' more cooking time. When it's done the fish should slide easily off the bone like a saucy little vixen, but if it doesn't, give it another minute or two. Serve with a lemon wedge.

Barry's Indian-spiced monkfish

Barry says

I'm blessed to have a really good Pakistani shop over the road from 147 Deli. We go over all the time and it's just amazing. There are brands he has there that I've never heard of before. You open them up and you can really smell the difference. Spices like that make a huge difference to a dish.

Monkfish is a beautiful meaty fish, so it can handle a strong marinade or a lot of flavour. It's like the pork of the fish world. It works so well on a barbecue and it can also take that charring on the outside. It's not a delicate fish – you can really batter the thing.

Serves 2–3

1 x 700g monkfish tail
Juice of 1 lime

For the marinade
4 tablespoons vegetable oil
2 tablespoons hot curry powder
1 tablespoon honey
½ tablespoon nigella seeds
1 teaspoon fenugreek seeds
1 teaspoon fine sea salt
1 teaspoon freshly ground black pepper
Zest and juice of 1 lemon
200ml coconut milk

You want to make the marinade either first thing in the morning or the night before you're going to be barbecuing.

Heat up your vegetable oil in a small saucepan over a medium heat and fry off the hot curry powder for 2–3 minutes. Add the honey, nigella seeds, fenugreek seeds, salt and pepper and stir to combine, then add the lemon zest and juice and coconut milk. Turn the heat down to low and bring the whole lot to a gentle simmer for 5 minutes, stirring regularly. Remove from the heat and let it cool completely.

Slather the monkfish in the marinade and leave it to absorb all the flavours for at least 6 hours, but preferably 12. Retain a bit of the marinade so you can brush the monkfish with it while it's on the barbecue.

When you're ready to barbecue, cook the monkfish tail over an indirect heat for 20 minutes, then for 6 minutes over the hot coals. Use the remaining marinade to brush it all over the tail as it cooks.

Squeeze over the lime juice before serving.

The perfect storm: The story of Dublin crab.

Nicola Brady

I didn't realise that a boat could tip over this far and not capsize. The waves of Dublin Bay are inky, dark and fighting with one another about which direction they want to go. As Howth slips away behind us, the horizon is anything but straight, slanting and tilting as the boat smashes over the waves.

The deck is slippery with saltwater and remnants of bait. The waves burst through the little gaps in the hull, drenching my shoes and legs as the spray from the surf soaks my face. As I cling onto a rope that hangs from the door of the wheelhouse, our photographer is behind me, treading precariously over the ropes that trail in neat lines along the deck, trying not to slide overboard with his camera in hand. Gaz has gone mysteriously, uncharacteristically quiet and is leaning over the side of the boat in a way that makes me think his breakfast has almost definitely reappeared.

But standing among us all, rolling a cigarette like he's propped up outside a pub on a sunny day, is Rob Markey, one of the fishermen. Looking at him, it's hard to believe he's on the same boat as us. I honestly believe he could stand on one foot, juggling crab pots, and there wouldn't be a bother to him. Next to him, we look like three people who have never stepped off dry land a day in our lives.

We're on our way to Lambay Island, a mysterious little isle off the Dublin coast that is known for two things: its resident herd of wallabies and the proliferation of delicious crab that are found just off its shores.

The man who is standing at the helm of the boat is Ger Markey, who has been fishing crab in these waters for decades. It's far from an easy job. Every day, these fishermen are at the mercy of the tides, the weather and the wind. They never know what they'll get once they throw the pots. If the weather is shit, they can't go out. Even when the weather is good, success is far from guaranteed.

A few days before we set out on the boat, Dublin had been baking in the heat in a stretch of unseasonably warm days. But while it made for great sailing, it absolutely destroyed the crab. 'It was perfect weather, but 30 degrees of heat,' says Ger. 'The crabs were dead in the box before we could even get back to the harbour. It's that quick. The boats here aren't set up for it because it doesn't happen that often. That was the perfect week for fishing, but we didn't get to do any.'

A more common weather-related obstacle? The wind. As our boat ricochets between the waves, Rob shouts out over the noise of the water. 'This is about force three to four today. If it was blowing four to five, we wouldn't be able to fish in this easterly wind. We could probably fish six to seven on a westerly wind because it's coming off the land.'

Something that may be surprising? Very few of the guys can swim.

This wind is most definitely not coming off the land. You can feel it blowing in from the sea, whipping around Ireland's Eye and battling in the channel between the land and the horizon.

But all that said, it's a rush to be out on the water, the bow of the boat battling through the swell and Lambay approaching in the distance, far bigger than I ever would have expected. When we pull up to a stop by their pots and stand well clear of the operations, it's a thrill to see it all in action.

One by one, the pots are hauled in. Seeing what's inside is a little like Christmas morning. The lads grade each crab by eye, quick as a whip, and throw the ones that are too small straight back in the sea. There are a few lobsters in the mix too, their bellies a bright sapphire blue that makes them look almost tropical. Gigantic starfish have made their way into the pots as well and I hold one in my hands for a few seconds, the little suckers gripping to my palms, before I pluck him off and release him back into the water.

A few velvet crabs make their way into the haul, their shells covered in a plush, thick matter that feels … well, it feels just like velvet. The crabs are popped into their crates, neatly organised to the side. The lobsters are kept in a separate crate. They're feisty little feckers, snipping away at each other like it's closing time at the bar.

When the pots are all in, it's time to throw the empty ones back. Rob has been stacking them in an organised, almost honeycomb pattern. I was admiring it for its neatness, but now I realise why they were placed in that way. When the anchor is thrown, the rope that connects all the pots pulls them back into the water, leaving them at an equal distance as the boat gently pulls away. By the time the anchor at the other end is cast, all the pots are lined up neatly on the seabed, ready for a new catch of crabs to move in.

It's a meticulous process. And it can only happen this fast, and this expertly, with the decades of experience that these guys have behind them. But even with all that expertise, the risks of this job are massive.

'This time two years ago, I was nearly dragged under by an anchor,' Ger tells me. 'The line came out of the hauler, the anchor went flying out and I went flying up in the air. I was going overboard and I grabbed onto the lever for the hauler as I went. It was spinning around and the ropes went back in. I was going overboard. I was dragged back into the hauler by my leg, upside down. Steven was with me. He ran up and only for that, my leg would have been gone. He knew.'

It's a knowledge that might seem obvious, but when things can turn deadly in a matter of seconds, there's no room for inexperience. And plenty of people wouldn't know what to do in that situation or how to act quickly enough to save a life.

'We'd often have young fellas out here and they wouldn't have a clue what they'd be doing,' says Ger. 'They'd stand there looking at you. I nearly lost my leg that day.'

Something that may be surprising? Very few of the guys can swim. Of the three I'm with, Ger and John Mooney can't, Rob can. Recently, tragedy almost struck when Ger was out fishing with Steven Farren, who can always be found with the lads getting lobsters.

'Steven fell in here one day. We were getting off the boat, I was down the back, and next of all I just heard a big splash. I says, "Where the fuck is he?" and I looked up. All I could see was the tail end of a splash in the water. I looked up and down the boat and he wasn't there. And I went, "No fucking way."

'I ran up the front of the boat. I just stood there, going, "I can't jump in after him because I can't swim." And he can't swim. I couldn't see him. The weight of the water in his oilskins had pulled him under. And next of all he came up. A pocket of air in his oilskins saved his life. He just floated to the top and started spinning around like a washing machine.

'I had to run around, come down and pull him in. Usually there are loads of people in the harbour. That evening, there was no one. Not a soul. I was screaming for help. If you're trying to lift a fella out of the water with wet clothes and wellies on, you just can't do it. We got him out in the end, but it was close. He went down to the bottom.

'He wears a life jacket every day. He only took it off because we were in the harbour. It was terrible. I was shook. I was helpless. Nobody was down here. I'd have drowned as well.

'It was all of 10 seconds. You ever hear that 10 seconds can change your life? That's what happened to me that day. It was 10 seconds. That was it.'

It's this level of risk, along with the hard physical toll, that means fewer and fewer people are entering the trade. These guys were all taught by their fathers. They followed into the family business, but the interest just isn't there anymore.

'Steven fell in here one day. We were getting off the boat, I was down the back, and next of all I just heard a big splash. I says, "Where the fuck is he?" and I looked up. All I could see was the tail end of a splash in the water. I looked up and down the boat and he wasn't there. And I went, "No fucking way."

'I ran up the front of the boat. I just stood there, going, "I can't jump in after him because I can't swim." And he can't swim. I couldn't see him. The weight of the water in his oilskins had pulled him under. And next of all he came up. A pocket of air in his oilskins saved his life. He just floated to the top and started spinning around like a washing machine.'

'I'll be the last one of my family,' says John. 'No kids have an interest in it now. There's no new blood coming into the industry. You won't find that many kids who want to get out of bed at half four in the morning.'

Rob agrees. 'I had a young fella that was out with me fishing for a day. He said never again. It was too much like hard work.'

'You're either making a fortune at this game or you're making nothing,' says Ger. 'There's no in-between. It's either a bad week or a good week. There's no all right week. But the good weeks are great.'

It's not unusual to hear of a fair few scraps on the docks too. One time, a 180,000-ton tanker anchored over their pots and cost them thousands. There are tales of divers sneaking down to nick lobsters out of them too. 'There'd be killings here at times,' Ger says. And I believe him.

Today's haul is a decent one. We've got a good group of crab and a few fat lobsters in the mix. From here, they go off to Derek Behan in Baldoyle, a perpetually joyful maestro who cracks all the crab with his prized spoon and a big beaming smile on his face. Whether the crab lands at midnight or early on a Sunday morning, it doesn't matter – he's straight in to sort it all out.

'He's a gentle soul,' says Gaz. 'He's always there with a massive smile on his face and his bright yellow gloves. He cracks the crab claws like he's a machine, hitting it with his spoon in exactly the right place, with such deft precision that the thick shell just falls away. It's like getting hit by Bruce Lee's one-inch punch. Without Derek's skilful hand on that end, it's all a fucking waste of time.'

From there, it's Rita's job to orchestrate the madness, pick up the crab and drive it straight down to the restaurant. She often brings Felix along for the ride and Derek will always throw him a few claws so that when he arrives at Michael's, he's got a massive grin on his face and his hands are full of crab shell.

The crab is boiled in the seawater it's caught in, which gives the crab you'll eat in Michael's an unparalleled level of flavour. Often the crab you eat in the restaurant was in the sea that morning.

'It's quite laborious and I don't think people realise that,' says Gaz as we pull into Howth Harbour. 'It can be a logistical nightmare too. But it's worth the extra step or two that we take to get this crab. Because we know that they care. And Derek cares as well. Customers can tell the difference. Once they've had this, they can't go back to fucking pasteurised shite.'

>
Derek Behan

But despite the back-breaking work, the curse of the weather, the fights on the dock and the risks at every turn, the passion that they all have for the job is clear as day.

'I still love it,' says Ger. 'You have to love it. If you didn't love it, you wouldn't do it. John's been at it 45 years and he's still here. You have to love it or you just wouldn't get out of bed in the morning. You see a few people who stick around when the money is good, but you have to be here when the money is bad as well. But it comes back around.'

'You have to take the good with the bad,' says John.

Later that day, we sit down in Michael's and the crab legs are on the plate in front of me, thick and sturdy and glistening with garlic butter. My jeans are still a little bit damp from the seawater, my face bright pink from the battering it took from the wind. And when I eat the crab, I feel like I can taste the sea. I've never had claws like them – firm and plump but soft as butter and so thick they almost take up my entire palm. I have never tasted crab as fresh in my life.

'It was the crab we had at the start of Michael's that set us apart,' says Gaz as he sucks the crab off the bone. 'And I genuinely mean that. We've built up this relationship for years. It would be way easier for Ger and Rob to just sell the crab to a truck driver and send it to China. But they don't because they care about what they do. And so do we. It can be a nightmare to organise and we can all do each other's heads in, but as wanky as it sounds, it's truly a labour of love.'

Meat.

Lamb shanks with dill, turmeric and chilli   81
Barry's lamb shoulder with mother sauce   82
Breaded lamb chops with zappy buttermilk dressing   85
Beef tartare, Austrian style   86
Pork porterhouse with salsa verde   88
Chicken thighs in a soy and mirin marinade   91
Chicken hearts in Jägermeister sauce   93
Bone marrow with mushroom vinaigrette   94
Flanken-cut beef ribs   97
Pheasant shepherd's pie   98
Barry's porchetta   102
Pork stelze   104
Roast pork belly with cumin and lime   106
Nenad's venison goulash   111
Lamb neck meatballs with a New York-style 'gravy'   112

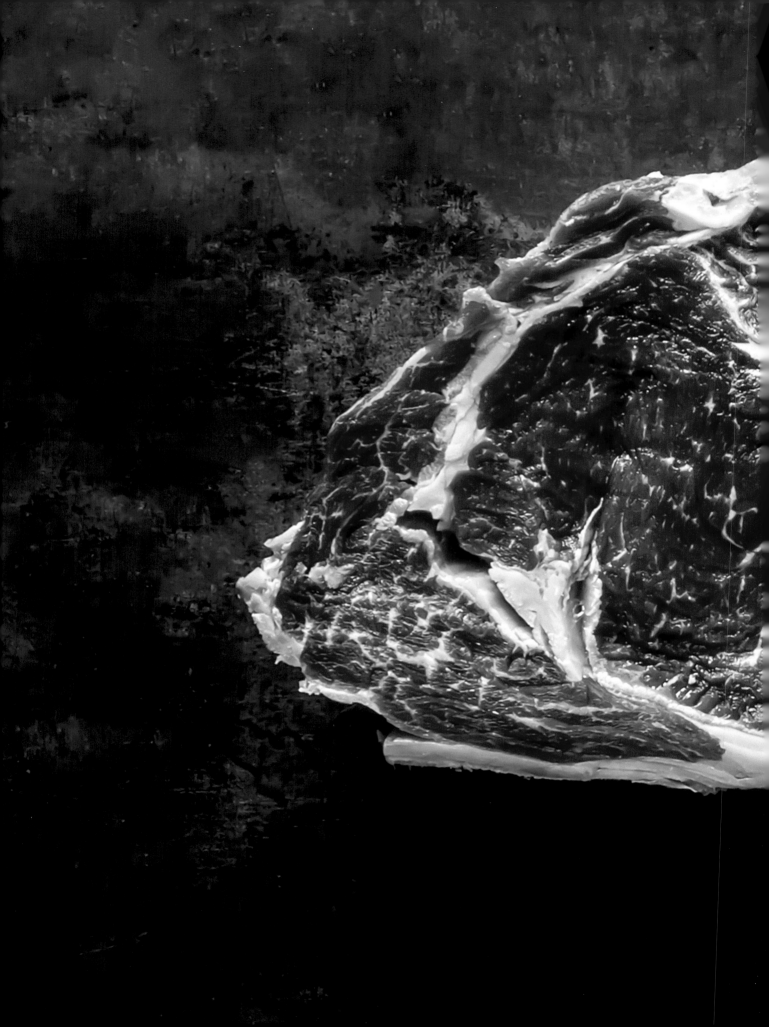

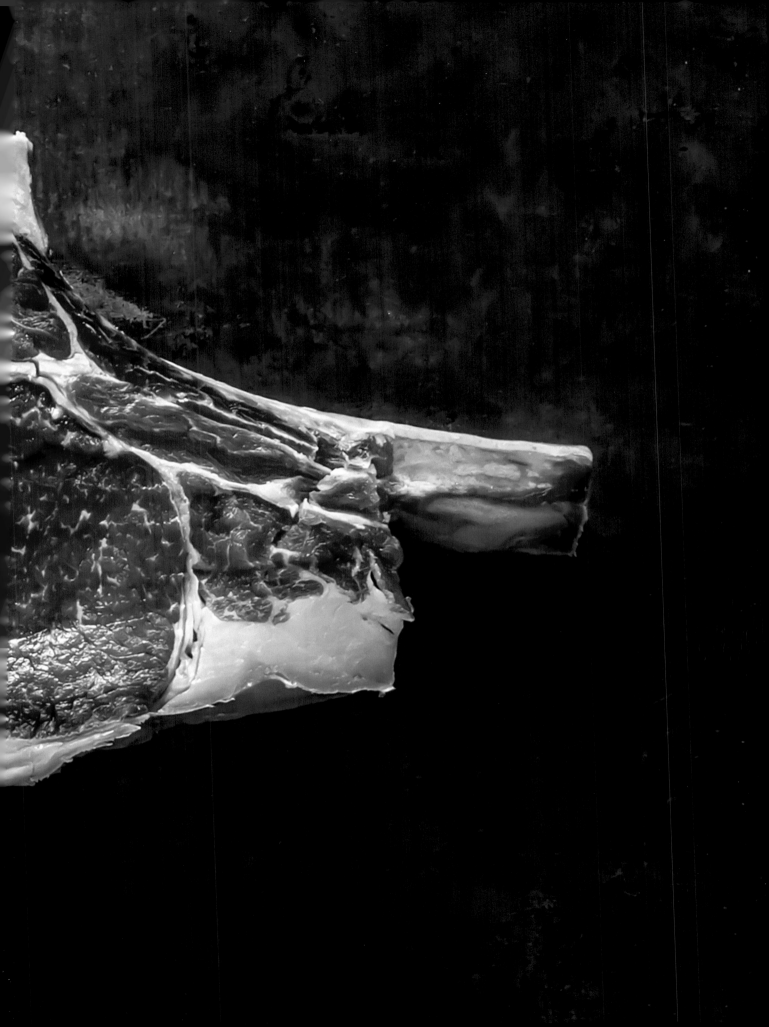

Lamb shanks with dill, turmeric and chilli

2 hind lamb shanks (see the chef's tip)
300ml beef stock

For the marinade
4 garlic cloves, minced
2 medium-heat fresh long red chillies, thinly sliced
(reserve some for garnish)
1 x 5cm cube of ginger, peeled and finely grated
80ml vegetable oil
2 tablespoons ground turmeric
2 heaped tablespoons chopped fresh dill
2 tablespoons fenugreek seeds
2 tablespoons crushed hazelnuts
1 tablespoon finely chopped fresh mint
4 good pinches of fine sea salt
2 good cracks of freshly ground black pepper

To garnish
Juice of 1 lemon
1 tablespoon chopped fresh dill
1 tablespoon finely chopped fresh mint
A handful of pistachios, shelled and roughly chopped

Preheat the oven to 200°C.

Put all the marinade ingredients into a mixing bowl and combine together well. You can also put this in a blender if you prefer.

Lightly score the skin of the lamb shanks using a small sharp knife in a criss-cross pattern, spaced 2.5cm apart. Rub the marinade all over the lamb, muttering, 'It puts the turmeric on its skin or else it gets the hose again' as you do.

Place the lamb shanks in a baking dish, casserole or a dish that you can cover tightly with tin foil. You need them to be well covered as they cook. Add the beef stock to the bottom of the dish or casserole and cover securely with the foil and/or a lid.

Roast the shanks in the oven for 1 hour, then reduce the temperature to 160°C and cook for a further 2 hours. If you want to nip off to the pub for a while, turn the oven down to 110°C and cook for 3 hours.

When you're ready to serve, give the lamb a final dressing with the lemon juice and scatter the dill, mint, pistachios and reserved chilli on top.

Gaz says
Lamb shanks have fallen out of fashion a little over the last few years, but I don't know why. They're super forgiving, lovely and tasty and they're foolproof to cook too. It's also a handy way to cook lamb for just one or two people without the faff of roasting a whole shoulder or leg. Just adjust the marinade accordingly.

Chef's tip
When you're getting the lamb shanks, ask for the hind legs. These have a much better fat and flavour content.

Serves 2

Barry's lamb shoulder with mother sauce

Barry says

Look, I'm not trained as a chef. I'm a cook. If you want to be technical, a mother sauce is one of five French classical sauces, which can then be turned into a Béarnaise or a mornay. But I don't know all the terms. For me, a mother sauce is just an all-rounder sauce that you can use on anything that takes your fancy.

You can chuck this sauce on just about anything. It's amazing as a marinade, but you can also brush some lamb chops with it as you put them on the grill and it'll be just as good. Put this on fish if you want. There are no rules here. When it comes to food, anyone who says you can't do something is a fucking idiot. It's like the people who say you can't have red wine with fish. Bullshit! You can do whatever the hell you want.

Serves 4–6

2kg free-range lamb fore shoulder
Sunflower oil
Fine sea salt and freshly ground black pepper

For the mother sauce
200g fresh flat-leaf parsley
200g fresh chives
100g fresh mint
80g capers
3 garlic cloves, peeled
300ml olive oil
Zest of 3 lemons and 100ml juice
2 tablespoons honey
50ml red wine vinegar
1 heaped teaspoon ground cumin
1 teaspoon chilli flakes

To serve
A squeeze of lemon

To make the mother sauce, blitz all the ingredients in a food processor or blender and store until ready to use.

To make the lamb, preheat the oven to 200°C.

Lightly score the skin of the lamb using a small sharp knife in a 2cm criss-cross pattern.

Rub a glug of sunflower oil all over the meat and put the lamb on a baking tray, then season well with salt (say, three good pinches) and a generous seasoning of pepper. Cover the tray securely with foil.

Roast in the oven for 45 minutes, then turn the heat down to 120°C and roast for a further 3–4 hours or as long as you want. Bear in mind, though, that if you cook it for longer than 4 hours, you'll need to turn the oven down to 100°C.

When you're ready to eat, turn the oven up to 220°C. Remove the foil, baste the lamb well and return it to the oven for another 20 minutes. At this stage, it'll be fully tender but whacking it under a high heat will give the lamb some colour.

Just before serving, drizzle the lamb with 6–7 tablespoons of mother sauce and a big squeeze of lemon.

Breaded lamb chops with zappy buttermilk dressing

Vegetable oil, for pan-frying
100g plain flour
2 eggs, whisked
150ml milk
100g panko breadcrumbs
8 spring lamb cutlets (see the chef's tip)
Fine sea salt and freshly ground black pepper

For the buttermilk dressing
125ml buttermilk
Juice of ½ lemon
4–5 tablespoons salsa verde (page 230)
2 teaspoons ground cumin
2 teaspoons toasted fennel seeds
2 teaspoons capers
2 big pinches of fine sea salt

First off, make the buttermilk dressing by whisking all the ingredients together. Set aside while you fry the cutlets to let the flavours all get to know each other.

Heat a good glug of oil in a large high-sided frying pan over a medium-high heat – you want the oil to be at least 1cm deep in the pan. When a few breadcrumbs dropped into the oil turn golden, you're good to go.

While that's heating up, get three wide, shallow bowls. Put the flour in the first bowl. In the second, whisk the eggs and milk together. Put the breadcrumbs in the third bowl.

Season the chops with salt and pepper. Toss each cutlet well in the flour, dusting off the excess before dipping them in the egg and milk mixture. Then dredge them in the breadcrumbs, pressing the crumbs into each chop to ensure they're all well covered with no bald spots.

You don't want to overcrowd the pan, so cook these in batches of four for 3 minutes on each side, until they're golden and crisp. (You can also do this in a deep-fryer at 180°C for 5 minutes in total.)

Drain them on kitchen paper and rest for 3–4 minutes. The lamb should be slightly pink in the middle.

When you're ready to serve, drizzle each chop with the buttermilk dressing and pop an extra bit on the table in case anyone wants to do a sneaky bit of dunking.

Gaz says
Let's face it – things fried in breadcrumbs are just better. If you leave anything around me for too long, chances are I'll coat it in breadcrumbs and lash it in a frying pan. And I'll regret nothing. Nothing, I say!

Everything about this dish is perfection. You've got the crunch from the crumb, the juiciness of the lamb and a good bit of tang from the buttermilk dressing. You don't need to serve these hot, either. They're actually even better when they're warm and they'd make a brilliant dish for a potluck dinner.

Chef's tip
This only works with a lamb cutlet, as gigot chops would be too gristly. It's got to be a rack of lamb with the French tips – you want each to be around 2–3cm thick and with a little fat on, but not too much. Your butcher will take care of all this for you or see the instructions in Rick's masterclass on pages 116–117.

Serves 2

Beef tartare, Austrian style

Gaz says

I always used to have beef tartare served in the French style, with capers and raw egg, and every time I ate it, I had to pretend that I enjoyed it. But to be honest, I was never a fan. It always just tasted like raw meat.

But everything changed when I went to Austria. There's a chef there, Christian Petz, who makes a tartare with a tomato dressing that's so much smoother. You're left with a dish that sings with flavour rather than just tasting like a mouthful of raw meat. We add in a bit of Worcestershire sauce and chilli for some heat and it's so, so good.

Chef's tip

When you're cutting up the beef, slice it against the grain and make the pieces as small as you can. Try to get rid of all the fat if you can.

Serves 2

150g very lean beef fillet per person, very finely chopped (see the chef's tip)
50g New York-style 'gravy' (see the recipe on page 228 or use good old-fashioned Dolmio)
25g sun-blushed tomatoes, finely chopped
1 small garlic clove, minced
1 teaspoon finely chopped capers in vinegar
1 teaspoon Worcestershire sauce
1 teaspoon horseradish sauce
1 teaspoon fish sauce
1 teaspoon red wine vinegar
2 good pinches of fine sea salt
A pinch of chilli flakes

For the avocado cream
1 ripe avocado, peeled and stoned
Juice of ½ lime
1 teaspoon mayonnaise
A good pinch of fine sea salt

To serve
Crusty ciabatta, thinly sliced and toasted

Put the beef, tomato sauce, sun-blushed tomatoes, garlic, capers, Worcestershire, horseradish, fish sauce, vinegar, salt and chilli flakes into a mixing bowl and combine well. Don't be scared to beat it up a little bit. The more you beat it, the lighter and smoother the tartare will be. Make sure you only mix this together when you're ready to serve, otherwise the vinegar and salt start to cook the meat.

To prepare the avocado cream, blend the avocado, lime juice, mayo and salt in a food processor (or use a stick blender) until you achieve a very smooth cream. Don't make this in advance, as the avocado turns brown in the blink of an eye.

To serve, plop 1 tablespoon of the avocado cream onto a plate. Top with the beef tartare and serve with toasted ciabatta. If you want to get really jazzy, you can mould the tartare with a scone-sized ring cutter. But it'll taste the same if you just dollop it on top of the avocado.

Pork porterhouse with salsa verde

Gaz says

A pork porterhouse is essentially a T-bone steak, but when it's from a cow, it's a steak, and when it's from a pig, it's a chop. There is, however, definitely a difference in the way you cook it. Pork isn't as forgiving as beef – while it's got the nice thick fat cap, it has very little fat actually going through the meat. It also cooks far quicker than you might expect.

I love pork for its richness and fattiness, but you need something sharp to cut through all that. This salsa has a load of really zesty, zingy, fresh flavours in it and they cut through it all perfectly. It's exactly what you want to serve with pork – something nice and zappy.

Chef's tip

This goes well with asparagus, tenderstem broccoli, spuds, rice or even a slice of bread. Have I mentioned that I quite like crusty white bread?

Serves 2

2 x 400g pork porterhouse chops
Fine sea salt and freshly ground black pepper
1 tablespoon butter
2 garlic cloves, thinly sliced
A handful of fresh flat-leaf parsley, finely chopped

To serve
2 tablespoons salsa verde (page 230)

Season your pork chops with salt and pepper. Score the fat three or four times – this will help the chops to stay flat on the pan and not curl up.

Heat a non-stick frying pan over a medium heat. Now this bit sounds complicated, but it isn't. With a pair of tongs, hold one chop in the hot dry pan, fat side down, and keep it there. A good pork chop should stand up on its own, but you don't want it to fall and splash you with hot oil. Sear the chop like this for 2–3 minutes, until the fat layer has rendered down and gone golden. You'll probably have to cook these one at a time, but no harm. They like a nice rest.

Once you've completed the above step, cook both the chops in the rendered fat over a medium-high heat for 4 minutes, until browned. Turn them over and repeat on the other side for a further 5 minutes, until browned and caramelised. Transfer each chop to a cutting board.

Take the pan off the heat and add the butter, garlic and parsley. When the butter has melted, pour all the buttery, fatty, garlicky juices over the chops. Take a moment to admire their beauty.

Cut the meat away from bone, then carve the meat into strips. Serve with a tablespoon of the salsa verde spooned on top of each porterhouse.

Chicken thighs in a soy and mirin marinade

8 boneless, skinless free-range chicken thighs, cut into strips
Seasoned flour, for dredging
Sunflower oil, for deep-frying

For the marinade
1 red onion, finely chopped
10 garlic cloves, peeled but left whole
A large pinch of coriander seeds (about 15 seeds)
20g cumin seeds
A handful of fresh flat-leaf parsley
100ml red wine vinegar
100ml mirin
75ml soy sauce
70ml sunflower oil
2 tablespoons fish sauce
2 tablespoons honey
1 teaspoon fine sea salt
2 teaspoons freshly ground black pepper

Put all the marinade ingredients into a blender and blitz until smooth. Reserve 4 tablespoons of the marinade for serving.

Put the chicken strips in a medium-sized bowl and pour over the marinade. Cover with cling film and marinate in the fridge for a minimum of 4 hours.

When you're ready to cook, heat the oil in a deep-fryer to 180°C. You can also do this in a big saucepan if you're really bloody careful about it.

Put the flour in a wide, shallow bowl and season it with salt and pepper. Dredge the marinated chicken strips in the seasoned flour, then deep-fry until they're golden brown, which should take 5–7 minutes.

To serve, drizzle the reserved sauce over the cooked chicken (obviously not the stuff that had raw chicken sitting in it for hours).

Gaz says
Once you taste this marinade, you'll want to make it by the truckload and take a bath in it every night. Or at the very least, drizzle it all over your naked lover. It's. Just. That. Good.

We initially tried simply marinating the chicken thighs, then whacking them under the grill, but they didn't char as much as I wanted them to. I wanted a really crisp skin to contrast with the sweet, sticky sauce. But that just didn't happen – the skin ended up claggy and flaccid, and nobody wants that. So we went with the fritti method, cutting the marinated thighs into strips and chucking them in a deep-fat fryer. That way, you get everything you want – a bit of crunch and succulent little morsels of chicken that make you want to keep eating, and eating, and eating, and eating …

**Serves 2 a main
or 4 as a starter**

Chicken hearts in Jägermeister sauce

200g whole free-range chicken hearts
A glug of vegetable oil, for pan-frying

For the sauce
50ml Jägermeister
Juice of ¼ large orange
3 tablespoons treacle
1 tablespoon fish sauce
1½ teaspoons freshly ground black pepper
1 teaspoon coriander seeds
½ teaspoon ground cinnamon
½ teaspoon fennel seeds
½ teaspoon garlic granules

To serve
A handful of fresh flat-leaf parsley, finely chopped
A squeeze of lime juice

Rinse the hearts with cold water and snip away any bits of fat or membrane from the crown. Cut the hearts almost in half lengthways, but don't go all the way through. You effectively want to butterfly them.

Add all the sauce ingredients into a large mixing bowl, whisking until the orange juice is fully blended with the treacle.

I prefer to pop the hearts on a skewer and barbecue them for 3 minutes on each side over a hot, direct heat. Alternatively, you can just chuck them onto a spanking hot frying pan with a dash of oil and cook for 2–3 minutes, stirring continually.

For the last 30 seconds of cooking, lash the sauce into the pan to deglaze, making sure all the chicken hearts get a good coating. If you're cooking them on a barbecue, reduce the sauce in a frying pan on a high heat for 40 seconds, then spoon it over the hearts.

Leave the hearts to rest for a minute or two before serving. When you're ready to eat, throw some chopped parsley, black pepper and a squeeze of lime juice on top and get ready to have your mind blown.

Gaz says
When we're plotting dishes for the restaurant, Rick and I always like to throw a few curveballs into the mix. We both love offering things that people won't have tried before and that they wouldn't ordinarily think to order. And it's worked out very well. As we always say, if you don't like it, there's no charge.

I think people like the bragging rights that come from trying cow's lips or tongue or heart. But it's not just for show – our customers know that they can trust us to make something that tastes damn good and isn't just a gimmick.

I'm well known for my love of Jägermeister, so there had to be a Jäger recipe somewhere in the book. But again, we didn't want this to look like stunt food. What we've created is a dish that is really, really good. We didn't want to hide anything or mask any flavours. We wanted to make a good, strong sauce that matches the pungent hearts. Eat this and you'll know you've just eaten chicken hearts and Jäger. There's no running from it – this flavour will punch you in the face.

Chef's tip
Make sure you rinse the hearts very well and make sure they have no odour at all. They should smell the same as a fresh chicken breast.

Serves 2

Bone marrow with mushroom vinaigrette

Gaz says

I bloody love bone marrow. You see it on so many menus in England, but I don't think we make enough use of it here. It's so, so good. Plus if people don't eat it, it just goes in the bin. It always makes me feel good when I can use all the parts of a cow. Ask your butcher to 'canoe' the bones for you by cutting them lengthways – you won't be able to do this at home.

This is one of those dishes that looks quite adventurous but is actually really easy. When you heat up the bone, the marrow melts like butter. You're then left with this unctuous, gelatinous, textured little delight that just sings with flavour. Pairing this with the earthiness of the mushrooms gives it a little something extra and the crispy onions add a bit of texture. But if you don't want to fuck around with the vinaigrette, try this with some parsley, thinly sliced raw onion and a bit of vinegar. I promise, you won't go back.

Chef's tip

If you want to get really jazzy, sprinkle some breadcrumbs on top for the last couple of minutes in the oven.

Serves 2

4 pieces of canoed bone marrow (i.e. two bones, both cut lengthways – see the intro)
Fine sea salt and freshly ground black pepper

For the mushroom vinaigrette

100ml sunflower oil
30g dried porcini mushroom powder (surprisingly easy to get)
1 sprig of fresh thyme if you have it to hand, leaves stripped
45ml red wine vinegar
10g fresh flat-leaf parsley, chopped

To serve

Crusty bread
A handful of fresh watercress leaves

Preheat the oven to 220°C.

To make the mushroom vinaigrette, put the oil, mushroom powder, thyme and a pinch of salt into a small pot and warm it gently over a medium heat to release all the mushroomy goodness from the powder. After 3 minutes, add the vinegar and give it all a good stir. Take it off the heat and stir in the parsley.

To cook the bone marrow, make little tin foil boats for the bones to sit in. That way, they stay standing up in the oven and don't fall over and drip precious marrow all over the oven tray. Season with a small pinch of salt, then roast the bones in their tin foil nests on a baking tray in the oven for 10–12 minutes. You want the marrow to be cooked all the way through but still fairly solid.

Top the marrow with the vinaigrette and serve with, you guessed it, some crusty bread and watercress. Give them a proper seasoning just before serving.

Flanken-cut beef ribs

Gaz says

When you get short ribs in a restaurant, they're cooked on the bone and it's an absolute beast. You'd never be able to fit the whole rack in your oven at home but when the short ribs are cut flanken style, the bones are cut cross-section so you're left with an easy-to-cook strip of ribs with small manageable bones. It's a little flavour sucker too. Any marinade you use gets into the meat much quicker because of the way it's cut. The texture is immense because they're cut across the grain, which means that each mouthful is a tasty, tender, gorgeous little dream of a thing.

Serves 3–4

1.3kg flanken-cut beef ribs

For the marinade
12 garlic cloves, minced
100ml vegetable oil
5 tablespoons chilli flakes
4 tablespoons soy sauce
3 level tablespoons fine sea salt
3 tablespoons freshly ground black pepper

To serve
2 tablespoons red wine vinegar

Whisk together all the ingredients for the marinade in a large bowl. Add the ribs and marinate them in this concoction, covered in cling film in the fridge, for at least 4 hours (but preferably 8 hours).

When you're ready to cook, preheat the oven to 220°C. Line a baking tray with greaseproof paper.

Pop the ribs (and all that delicious marinade) into the tray. Cook in the oven for 20 minutes, then reduce the temperature to 160°C and continue to cook for a further 30 minutes. Flip the ribs around and cook for a final 30 minutes.

Just before serving, give the ribs a good drizzle of red wine vinegar.

Pheasant shepherd's pie

Gaz says

Right. I know this might look like a bit of a faff to make, but it's so fucking good. It might even be my favourite recipe in the whole book. This is the perfect thing to make on a drizzly Sunday when you just want to spend the whole day pottering around the kitchen, beer in hand, as the smells flittering out of the oven get better and better as the day goes on.

Pheasant has such a distinct flavour. It loves being paired with something smoky, like pancetta, to fight with that powerful flavour a little bit. Combine the gamey pheasant with that smokiness, a kick from the mustard and a crunchy, golden rosti top and you're in flavour country. But if you can't get hold of pheasant, you can make this with a simple roast chicken. I'd much rather you do this with chicken than not make it at all.

Chef's tip

Don't squish the rosti topping down – you want to keep it feathery and light or the heat won't penetrate down into the dish. Pack it too tight and you end up with a rosti that's black on the outside and raw in the middle.

Serves 4

For the pie filling

6 tablespoons vegetable oil
5 pheasant breasts, cut into 3 pieces (or 1 whole chicken)
1 small brown onion, finely diced
4 small to medium carrots, peeled and finely diced
1 leek, thinly sliced and rinsed
2 garlic cloves, minced
100g pancetta lardons
600ml chicken wing gravy (page 227)
A small handful of fresh flat-leaf parsley, finely chopped
Leaves from 4 fresh rosemary stalks, finely chopped
2 tablespoons wholegrain mustard
2 tablespoons Dijon mustard
2 tablespoons Worcestershire sauce

For the rosti

400g peeled Rooster potatoes
100g finely chopped onion
75g butter, melted
3 free-range egg yolks
1 tablespoon Dijon mustard
A handful of fresh flat-leaf parsley, finely chopped
A few fresh thyme leaves
2 large pinches of fine sea salt
4 grinds of freshly ground black pepper

Preheat the oven to 200°C.

Heat 2 tablespoons of the oil in a large frying pan on a medium heat. Add your pheasant and cook until browned, then set aside. If you're using a chicken, roast it in the oven for 1 hour.

Now start the rosti mix. Grate the potatoes and soak them in a bowl of cold water for at least half an hour to get rid of the starch. Feel free to change the water after 15 minutes.

Next up is the pie filling. In a large saucepan, heat the remaining 4 tablespoons of oil on a medium heat. Add the onion, carrots, leek, garlic and pancetta and gently sweat it all down until the veg is soft, then add the chicken wing gravy. Remove the pan from the heat and set aside.

If you're using chicken, pick the meat off the bones and roughly chop it up. You can leave the skin on if you like. Otherwise, your browned pheasant is hot to trot.

Fold the meat into the gravy and vegetable mix, then stir in the herbs, mustard and Worcestershire. Spread it all into a baking dish – a lasagne dish will do the trick nicely. Leave this to cool slightly while you fiddle with the potatoes.

Squeeze all the water out of the grated potato as best you can. You can put it in a clean tea towel if you like, but you need to put some muscle into it. The drier the potato, the better the dish will be.

Add the onion, melted butter, egg yolks and mustard to the potato along with the parsley, thyme, salt and pepper. Give it a really good stir.

Put the potato mix on top of the pheasant (or chicken) but don't press it down. Remember, you need to keep it fluffy and feathery, with a bit of height. If it's too flat, the spuds will sink into the gravy. Grind two big turns of pepper onto the top of the spuds and pop it into the oven. Cook for 25 minutes, until the potato is nice and golden on top.

Eat!

Barry's porchetta

Barry says

You want to keep a porchetta really simple – you don't want to put much in the way of it. I don't even know if mine is a traditional porchetta stuffing, but it's really good. And everything is better with stuffing, right? I want this stuffing to really punch you in the face with flavour. It's got to go toe to toe with 3 kilos of pork and still be tasty enough for sandwiches the following day if there are any leftovers – and that's a big if.

You can eat this porchetta as is, but it works so well in a sandwich. I'd use nice bread, good butter and maybe some really thinly sliced fennel tossed in apple cider vinegar and a little bit of watercress. Perfect.

Chef's tip

You can make the stuffing at home and bring it to your butcher and ask them to roll and tie the porchetta for you. Just make sure they weigh the meat before the mix goes in (but don't tell Rick I said that).

**Serves 4–6
(with enough left over
for sandwiches)**

1 x 3kg piece of pork loin with the belly still attached (tell your butcher you're making porchetta and they'll know exactly what you need)

For the stuffing
200g butter
2 large white onions, finely diced
2 large fennel bulbs, thinly sliced
6 garlic cloves, minced
3 tablespoons toasted fennel seeds
Fine sea salt and freshly ground black pepper
150ml white wine
150g fresh flat-leaf parsley, finely chopped
20 fresh sage leaves, chopped
Zest of 2 lemons

Melt the butter in a large saucepan over a medium heat. Add the onions, fennel and garlic along with the toasted fennel seeds. Season lightly with salt and sweat down until the onion and fennel are softened but not coloured.

Throw in your wine and simmer the whole lot for 5 minutes. Season again with salt and pepper.

Remove the pan from the heat and stir in the parsley, sage and lemon zest. Leave to cool, then store in the fridge until you're ready to use.

To cook the porchetta, preheat the oven to 180°C.

Roll the porchetta and tie it securely – you can see how Rick does this on pages 120–121. Place on a baking tray and put tin foil at both sides of the porchetta to keep the stuffing in. Roast in the oven for 40 minutes, basting it halfway through.

Turn the oven up to 220°C and roast for 25 minutes more, basting it again when that time is about halfway up.

Leave to rest before carving into slices and either eating it as is or in a sandwich. Spoon over the juices from the roasting tray after carving or serve in a small dish on the side.

Pork stelze

Gaz says

You may not have heard of this before, but it's a classic in Germany and Austria. Basically, a stelze is the pork shank, or the hock that hasn't been cured – it's also called the knuckle. It's so easy to make, but Jesus, it's so good. All that skin on the outside makes for the most amazing crackling, a full filthy circle of it that encases the whole thing like a big crackling cuddle. And the meat inside? It's like butter.

There's a place in Vienna called Schweizerhaus and all they really serve is these pork stelze and pints of beer. That's it. If there were four of you, you'd get four beers, a stelze in the middle of the table and you'd all just mill into it. It's how you'd spend a sunny Sunday, sitting with this and nibbling away to your heart's content.

We usually serve this with our sneaky sauerkraut (page 203) and dumplings or spuds. If you were serving it as the main course for four people, you'd want two of them. But if you're just sitting with a few beers and tipping away at it, one stelze would do four people. If you were feeling greedy, you'd have one each. And nine beers. Which I have done before. For breakfast. On a Monday.

Chef's tip

Uncured pork hocks aren't always found in the butcher, but a good one will be able to hold a couple back for you before they turn them into ham hocks. They can also score them for you if you like.

Serves 2

For the stelze
1 uncured pork hock (see the chef's tip)
Fine sea salt

Score the skin of the hock in a criss-cross pattern, roughly 1cm apart (about a finger's width) all the way around. This is key, as it will allow the skin to crisp up nicely and turn into a golden, sweet crackling while sheltering all the juicy meat inside. You can give the skin a few jabs with a sharp fork or skewer too. The more 'drainage' that allows the fat to escape, the better the crackling will be.

Massage salt liberally all over the skin and into all the nooks and crannies of the hock, like you were massaging your lover on their birthday. Let it sit for 1 hour.

Preheat the oven to 200°C.

Place the hock on a baking tray, bone side up, and cook in the oven for 45 minutes to crisp up the skin.

Turn the oven down to 120°C and cook for 90 minutes more to gently cook the inside.

After the 90 minutes are up, check the hock. Each one is different, so you might need to whack the oven up to 200°C again to make sure the crackling is good and crisp. The meat inside is very forgiving, so don't worry about overcooking it. Your focus should be on the skin – the crackling maketh the stelze.

Take the hock out of the oven and rest for 10–15 minutes before serving. Try to resist the temptation to sneak pieces of the crackling for yourself as you hide in the kitchen, gently sobbing over your lack of self-restraint. Because pretty soon the whole lot will be gone and you'll have a hell of a lot of explaining to do.

Roast pork belly with cumin and lime

Gaz says

If you ever want to make a nice Sunday dinner without cooking a roast, this is the dish to make. It ticks all the boxes – it's nice and juicy, succulent as anything and really forgiving. You can chuck this in the oven and forget about it until you're ready to sit down and go to town on some pork. I love cooking with the forgiving cuts of meat like cheeks, shoulders and belly. To me, home cooking shouldn't be stressful. It should be about minimum effort and maximum flavour. Which is this recipe in a nutshell.

I love the combination of pork and cumin, but with this dish you need at least four times the amount of cumin that you'd think you need. The seeds look stronger than they are, so don't be afraid to lash them all on. Their power dissipates as the dish cooks and the whole seeds are far more fragrant than they are strong.

Serves 4 (with leftovers for sandwiches the next day)

2kg free-range pork belly
½ large onion
130ml sunflower oil
30g cumin seeds
20g fennel seeds
5g coriander seeds
10g fine sea salt
10g freshly ground black pepper
6–7 sprigs of fresh thyme

To serve
2 limes, halved

Preheat the oven to 200°C.

Place the pork on a clean chopping board and score the skin in a criss-cross pattern with a sharp Stanley knife. Be sure to cut the fat, not the flesh. You can see Rick do this on page 120.

Using a small sharp knife, jab the skin all over to allow the fat to drain – this means you'll get a nice crisp crackling.

Place the onion half in a large metal baking tray, cut side up, and place the pork on top. This creates an arch to support the pork and allows the fat to pour off, again to give you a banging crackling.

Combine the oil, seeds, salt and pepper in a bowl, then rub this all over the pork skin, making sure to get it in every little crevice. Lash the whole thyme sprigs into the tray too.

Cover the tray tightly with tin foil. Cook in the oven for 30 minutes, then reduce the temperature to 160°C and continue cooking for a further hour. If you're going to leave it alone for a while, reduce the temperature to 110°C, then you're as free as a bird for however long you fancy.

When you're almost ready to eat, remove the tin foil and scrape up any of the sauce that's fallen into the tray. Baste the pork with any of the seeds or fat that have seeped off. You only want to use the fat to get a good crackling – if you use any of the juices, it will make your crackling soggy. If you tilt your tray, you should see a difference between the fat and the stock that pool in the corner – gently lift out the fat with a spoon, leaving the stock in the pan. You're only looking to use a tablespoon or two of the fat.

Whack the heat up to 200°C and roast for 30 minutes to an hour, until you have perfect, smackable crackling. You can do this under a grill if you prefer.

When you're ready to serve, carve the pork and cover the whole lot in a generous squeeze of lime juice. Spoon the roasting juices over the meat too.

Nenad's venison goulash

4 tablespoons sunflower oil

1 x 1kg venison haunch, cubed

750g onions, finely chopped

300g carrots, peeled and chopped

200g pancetta, cubed

500ml red wine

500g ripe tomatoes, finely chopped

5 garlic cloves, finely chopped

1 litre beef stock

4 tablespoons red wine vinegar

5 tablespoons good-quality paprika

2 tablespoons sweet paprika

A pinch of caster sugar

Fine sea salt and freshly ground black pepper

A handful of chopped fresh flat-leaf parsley

100g sour cream

To serve

Buttered gnocchi

Heat 2 tablespoons of the oil in a large saucepan over a medium heat. Fry off the venison in batches until it's brown.

In another pan, heat the other 2 tablespoons of oil over a medium-low heat. Add the chopped onions and sweat gently for 10 minutes, stirring regularly. As they start to soften, turn the heat down to low and cook for 20 minutes more. Add the carrots and pancetta and cook for a further 10 minutes.

Deglaze the venison pan with the red wine, scraping up all the good bits from the bottom of the pan. Drink the 250ml of wine that's left in the bottle for absolutely crucial quality control. Yes, quality control.

Add the chopped tomatoes, garlic, stock, vinegar, paprika, sugar and six pinches of salt to the pan. Bring to the boil, then reduce the heat, add the venison and simmer, uncovered, over a low heat for 2 hours so that the sauce thickens and reduces slightly.

Season to taste with salt and pepper and stir in the chopped parsley, then plop a dollop of sour cream into each bowl. This pairs really well with buttered gnocchi.

Gaz says

This is a recipe from Nenad (affectionately known as Neno), who works in Michael's. I've been friends with Neno for nearly 20 years at this stage and he's been in the restaurant since day one. Simply put, he's my rock in there.

Neno is from the Croatian coast and has been cooking since age 11. He always jokes that if you're big enough to ride a bike, you're big enough to go work in a restaurant for the summer tourist season. Everyone there has their own recipe for a goulash that's been passed down from their granny. It's the kind of recipe that people will argue over – everyone makes it in a slightly different way and everyone believes that theirs is the best, kind of like the way we are with our Irish stew. But Neno's really is the best.

Serves 4–6

Lamb neck meatballs with a New York-style 'gravy'

Gaz says

We were originally planning on doing a lamb neck burger for the book, but it just didn't work. It was too fatty – and that's coming from me. I love the idea of some kind of lamb concoction in bread, though, and these work really well in a sub. The fat in the lamb makes for an absolutely banging meatball and the whole thing is heaven in a bun. But you can also have them on their own or with some nice pasta.

When we make these in Michael's we use a blend of lamb, beef and pork that we mince ourselves, but your butcher can always make you up a little blend if you bat your eyelashes at them.

Serves 4

600g minced lamb neck (ask your butcher for around 30% fat)
1 egg, beaten
1 egg yolk
25g panko breadcrumbs
100ml milk
1 tablespoon dried oregano
1 tablespoon garlic granules
1 teaspoon sweet paprika
2 big pinches of chopped fresh flat-leaf parsley
1½ teaspoons fine sea salt
2 pinches of freshly ground black pepper
4 tablespoons vegetable oil

To serve
400ml New York-style 'gravy' (page 228) or tomato sauce

Mix together all the meatball ingredients except the vegetable oil in a large bowl. With clean hands, make golf ball-sized meatballs from the mix – you should get around 15 balls.

Heat up the vegetable oil in a large frying pan over a medium-high heat.

It's time to add your balls to the frying pan. You can cook them in batches if your pan is on the smaller side, but once the meatballs are in the pan, don't touch them for 5 minutes. If you do, they will fall apart in the pan. You want to get a crust forming on your balls. And this is the only time in your life that you want that. Once they're nicely seared, you can turn them over and cook for another 5 minutes.

Add the New York-style 'gravy' or tomato sauce to the pan. Pop a lid on the pan, turn down the heat to low and gently simmer for 25 minutes – don't simmer for too long, as you want to keep the balls nice and juicy. If your frying pan can go into the oven, you can pop it in there at 180°C for 15 minutes.

Serve these warm and on their own, with pasta or inside soft white bread rolls with some grated mozzarella melted on top. Whatever you fancy. These are your balls, so do whatever you want with them.

Rick's butchery masterclass.

You might prefer to leave everything to your butcher, but if you want to try your hand at a bit of butchery at home, Rick has you covered.

Here are his four tutorials with everything to get the home butcher started.

How to French trim a rack of lamb

Chef's tip
Don't throw away any of the delicious trim – the fat can be used to cook with another time, while the trim and bones can be used to make a delicious stock or broth.

Step 1
Remove the chine bone (backbone) carefully with a saw or ask your butcher to do this for you (they will have all the necessary tools). Carefully and slowly make long strokes with the saw along the end of the ribs nearest to the chine bone. Do this slowly so you don't damage the eye of the rack of lamb.

Step 2
Using a boning knife, gently follow the shape of the chine bone, loosening it as you go. Use your left hand to pull the bone away from the meat – this will help you to have a clear view of the position of the tip of your knife.

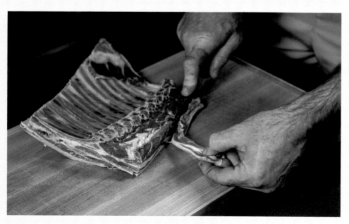

Step 3
Remove the elastin strap from underneath the chine bone. Using your knife, make a long straight cut between the elastin and the eye of the meat.

Step 4
Flip the rack of lamb bone side down and make a long straight cut about 5cm from the top of the ribs. Carefully run your knife along the back of the meat, keeping your knife close to the ribs to remove the excess meat and fat along the back of the ribs.

Step 5
Stand the lamb upright and make a cut down each side of the ribs, only as far as the line you made when removing the meat along the back of the ribs. Now nick the meat in between the ribs to remove this meat.

Step 6
Remove the back fat if desired – personally I leave it on, but in order for breadcrumbs to stick properly, it's better to remove it. Starting at the top, slowly run your knife along the fat to loosen it ever so slightly. With one hand, press your palm down over the remaining back fat and with the other gently pull the fat where you have made the incision. Do this gently so as not to damage the eye of the meat.

How to prepare a prime rib of beef

Before you start

Have your butcher remove the chine bone or use the steps set out in removing the chine bone from the rack of lamb on page 116.

Chef's tip

Don't throw away any of the delicious trim – the fat can be used for cooking and the trim can be used for the smash burgers on page 176 if you're lucky enough to have a small home mincer or grinder. The bones can be used to make a delicious stock or broth.

Butcher's tip

Source your beef carefully. Ask your butcher for an Angus or Hereford cut (which are commonly found) with a nice fat and marble score because fat = flavour. Try to avoid Continental breeds of cattle for this cut (such as Limousin or Charolais) because they tend to be very lean animals.

Step 1

Flip the beef bone side down and make a long straight cut about 5cm from the top of the ribs. Carefully run your knife along the back of the meat, keeping your knife close to the ribs, to remove the excess meat and fat along the back of the ribs.

Step 2

Stand the beef upright and make a cut down each side of the ribs, only as far as the line you made when removing the meat along the back of the ribs. Now nick the meat in between the ribs to remove this meat.

Step 3

Remove the back fat if desired. Personally I remove it because it tends to have a different texture than the rib-eye. Note that this rib cap is not the rib-eye cap (*spinalis dorsi*). The *spinalis* is still attached to your rib-eye.

Start from the top and gently run your knife along the fat, loosening it ever so slightly. With one hand press your palm down over the remaining back fat and with the other gently pull the fat where you have made the incision in order to separate the back fat from the meat. Do this gently so as not to damage the eye of the meat.

How to stuff and roll a porchetta

Before you start
Have your butcher remove the chine bone or use the steps set out in removing the chine bone from the rack of lamb on page 116.

Step 1
Gently slide your knife along the inside of the ribs while angling the knife slightly towards the rib bones. This will keep as much meat on the joint as possible. You don't need to be too fussy about this because leaving a little meat on the ribs for cooking at a later stage is definitely not the end of the world.

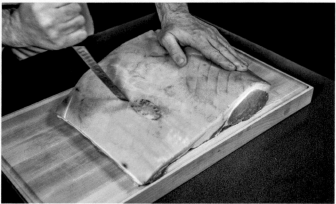

Step 2
Using a Stanley knife or a very sharp blade, score the skin diagonally from left to right. Do this gently – you want to penetrate the skin but not the meat. Turn the meat around and repeat the process so you are left with diamond scores about 2cm apart.

Step 3
Flip the meat over so the skin is facing down. At the eye end of the loin, carefully butterfly the eye with your knife but only halfway through. Flip it over and press it out with your hands so you have an even thickness all the way along the meat.

Step 4
Apply your stuffing as desired all the way along the meat.

Step 5
From the eye end, roll the whole joint up like one big carnivorous Swiss roll.

Step 6
Tie it up using a butcher's knot. Google it or look up how to make a butcher's knot on YouTube – we confess that words failed us on how to explain this one.

How to spatchcock a chicken

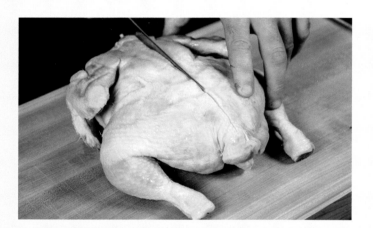

Step 1

Place your chicken breast side down. With your knife, make an incision along the whole length of the backbone.

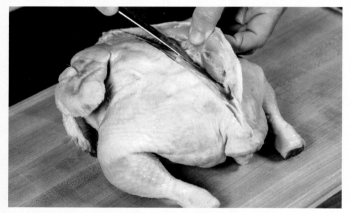

Step 2

Gently start to follow the shape of the ribs with your knife on both sides until you are halfway down the ribs.

Step 3

When you reach the leg joints, apply a little pressure with the tip of your knife to penetrate in between the leg joint.

Step 4

Turn your chicken so the legs are facing towards you. Place your middle finger in the neck hole and pull upwards towards yourself while holding the rest of the carcass on the surface to remove the back of the bird.

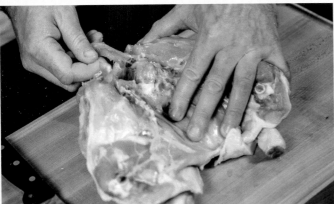

Step 5

Break the wishbone off on each side. Be careful because it can be sharp.

Step 6

Hold your knife along the now exposed breastbone and gently tap the top of the blade (obviously not the sharp side) just to crack the breastbone ever so slightly.

Step 7

Flip the bird so the breasts are pointing up. Using the palm of your hand, gently press on the breastbone to further crack it. This way the chicken lays flat for better and more even cooking results.

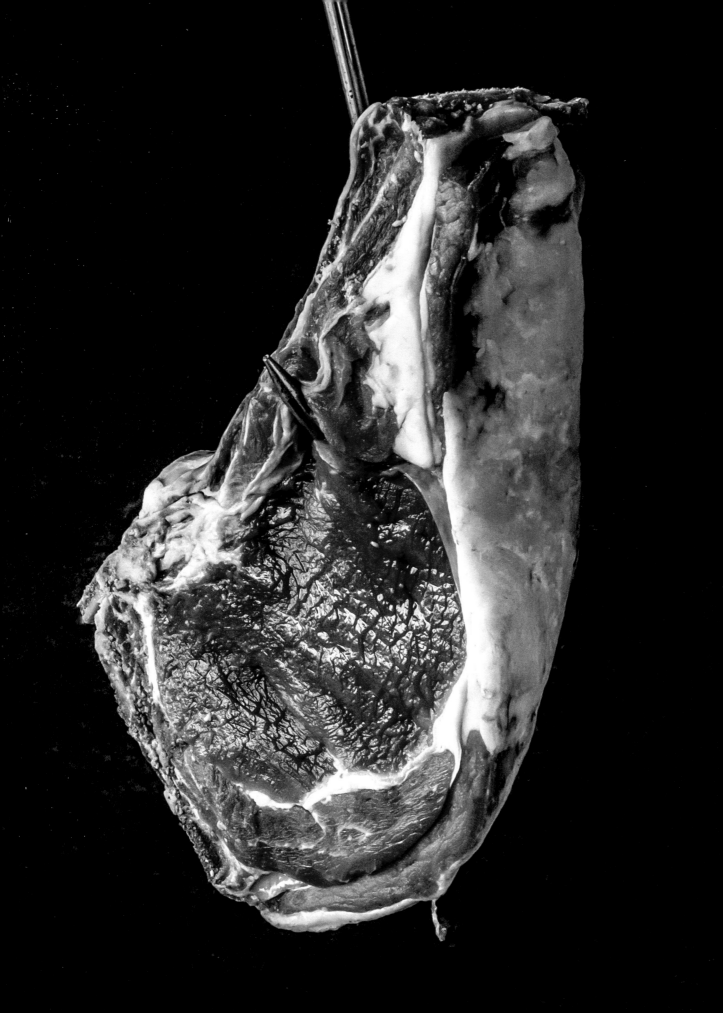

Steaks and reverse searing.

Picanha   130
Fillet on the bone   132
Hanger   134
Reverse-seared rib of beef   136

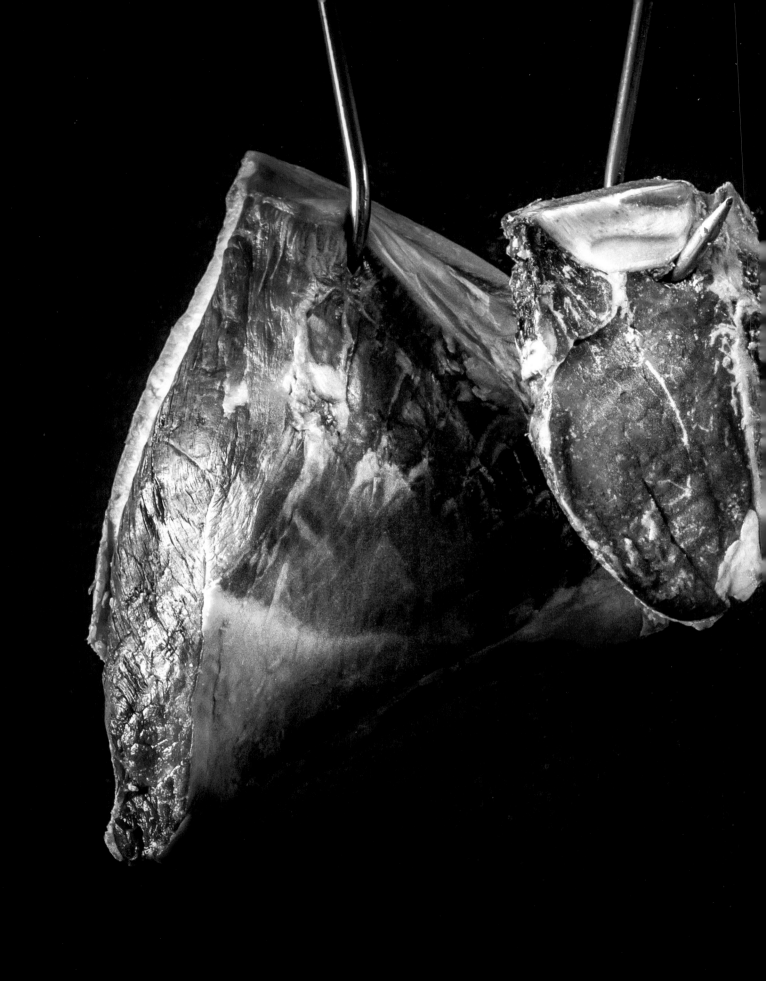

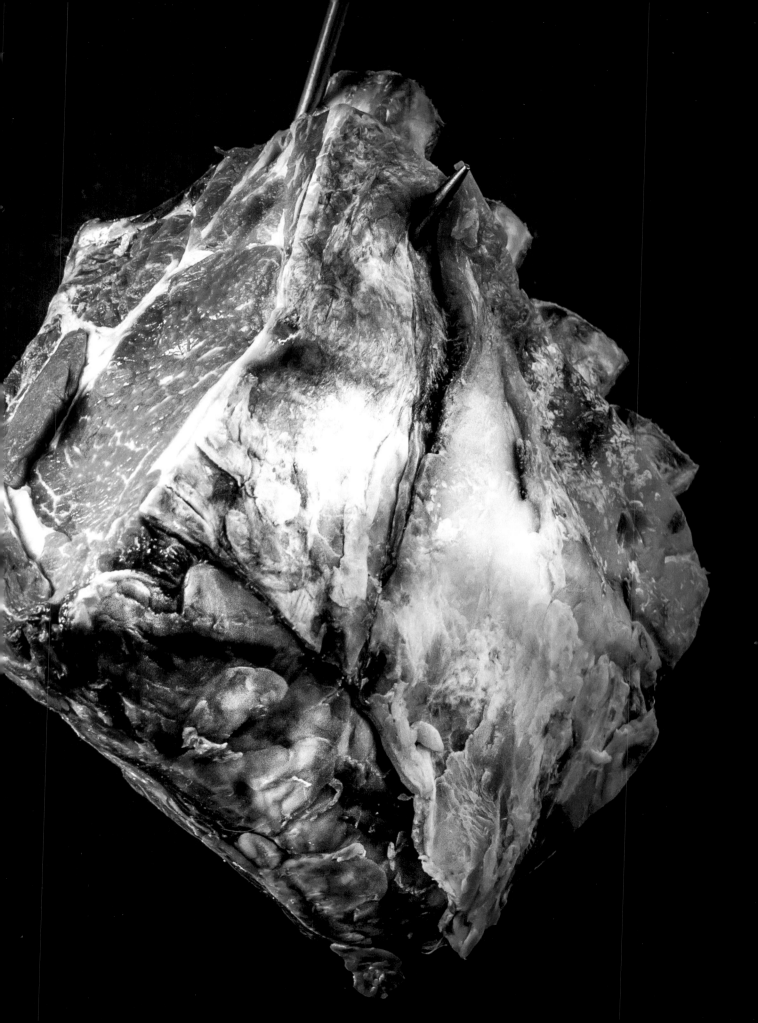

How to cook a steak.

No matter the cut, there are a few golden rules when it comes to cooking a steak. First off, you need to bring your meat to room temperature, so take it out of the fridge at least an hour before cooking it and season it well. The sign of a good steak is one that can stand up on its own, so opt for a big fat one. If you're feeding two people, it's better to have one thick steak than two skinny ones.

Get a frying pan spanking hot. The first part of the steak to touch the pan should be the fat – use a pair of tongs to hold it against the hot pan so that the fat renders out nicely. Once you've put the meat down on the pan, don't touch it. Leave it to get a nice char. Ideally, you should turn the steak only once. You can throw in a knob of butter right at the end for flavour and use a spoon to toss that lovely melted butter over the top of your steak as it finishes cooking. Give it a good long rest before carving and eating, particularly if it's a big steak for two.

Every single steak is different and no one cooking time fits all. When you're buying a steak, have a chat with your butcher and see what they recommend in terms of prep. But however you're cooking it, whether it's on a barbecue or in a pan, the most important bit of kit you can have is a digital meat probe thermometer. That way, you're left with a perfectly cooked steak every time.

Beef temperature cheat sheet
When using your magical meat probe, all the guesswork is taken out of cooking a steak. This is the best tool you can have in your arsenal. Remember, the internal temperature continues to rise a little when it's resting, so always take your meat off the heat when it's a couple degrees cooler than your desired temperature.

Rare: 50°C (so remove it at 48°C)
Medium rare: 55°C (so remove it at 52°C)
Medium: 60°C (so remove it at 58°C)
Medium well: 65°C (so remove it at 63°C)
Well done: 70°C (so remove it at 68°C)
Very well done: Get the hell out of here.

Picanha

Rick says

There's nothing quite like a picanha. It's always been popular in South America, but it's becoming increasingly popular over here and it's easy to see why. The flavour off it is just immense thanks to the big layer of fat that sits right on the top. That epic fat cap is what makes this one stand out, so make sure the picanha you buy has a lovely thick layer of fat on it or it simply won't work.

Remember the golden rule: fat = flavour.

It works really well on the barbecue – a picanha loves a good char. When that fat is blackened on the coals, it just ramps the flavour up even more. But it also works well in the oven and it is a really good contender for the reverse searing method.

As with all beef, remove it from the fridge a couple hours before cooking to allow the meat to come up to room temperature. Salt it generously.

If you're reverse searing, use the method on pages 136–137.

If you're cooking it on the barbecue, start on a high heat, meat side down. Sear it for 3–4 minutes, then flip it to fat side down. Cook for another 3–4 minutes and watch out for flare-ups (when the fat drips onto hot coals and creates a big flame). If that happens, just move the meat to the side where the coals aren't as hot.

Lower your barbecue temperature and close the lid. (Remind me to tell you the story sometime of when Gaz opened the lid of a barbecue only to singe his eyelashes, eyebrows and hair on a massive fireball.)

Keep cooking until you reach your desired temperature. I'd recommend no more than a medium cook for this (so remove the steak from the heat when it hits 58°C internally).

Much like me, a picanha loves a good long rest. The secret to a great picanha is to always allow for a rest that's almost as long as the total cooking time.

When you're carving, be sure to cut against the grain. This way you get the best possible texture and eating experience.

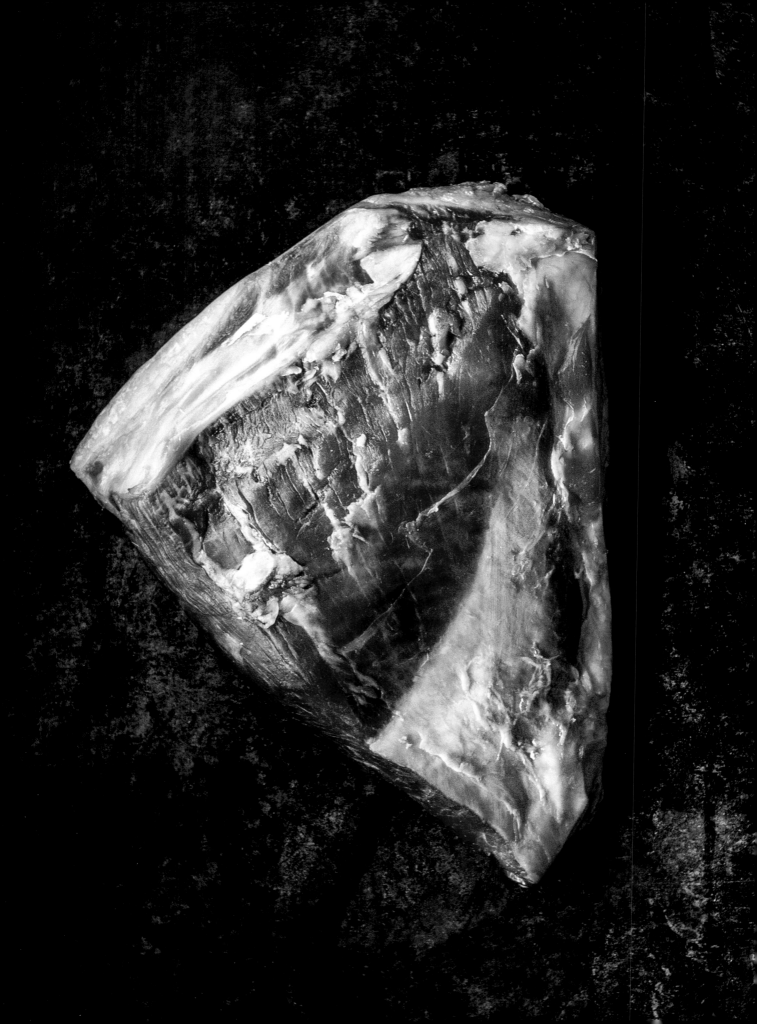

Fillet on the bone

Rick says

To be honest, I'm not really a fan of fillet steak. I think it lacks flavour, especially compared to something like a rib-eye. But keep a fillet on the bone and everything changes. Leaving the bone in is an absolute game changer, especially if it's been dry aged. Suddenly, you've got a steak that's packed with complex flavours and a hefty smack of deliciousness. If you walk into a butcher shop and they've got fillet on the bone, you know that's a real butcher.

Carefully sourced fillets are always going to be tender, so what you're really on the lookout for is a little bit of marbling (bear in mind you'll only get a small amount of marbling in a grass-fed fillet). Like all good things in life, you want one that's sturdy, not flaccid, and holds its shape at the critical time.

They're really simple to cook. Bring it to room temperature and season generously with sea salt.

Get your meat probe and insert it horizontally (never vertically) in the middle of the steak.

Cook it on a very hot pan or barbecue until it reaches your desired temperature (see our handy cheat sheet on page 129).

Allow it to rest for 10 minutes (practising all your self-restraint) and then devour it.

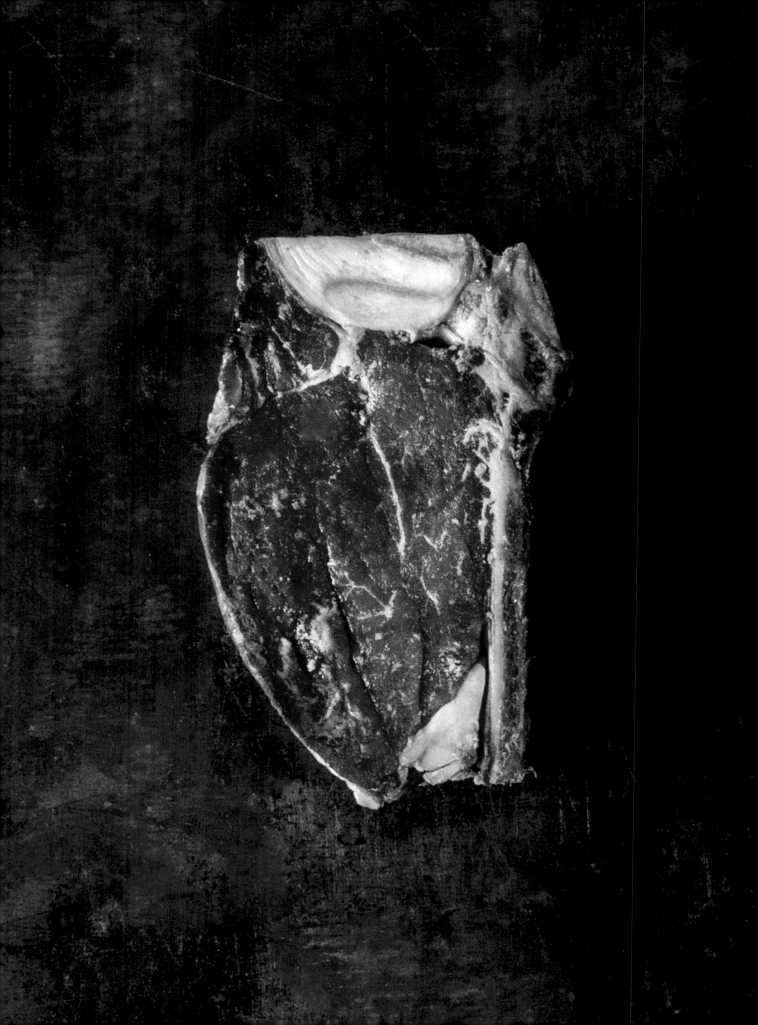

Hanger

Rick says

The story behind the hanger is a bit of a mindblower. There's only one tiny little hanger per animal, weighing in at 600–700g. When you consider that the average heifer carcass can be up to 300kg, suddenly the hanger looks a little bit like a pearl hiding in an oyster. Traditionally, it was always known as a butcher's treat because they'd nab it to take it home for their own dinner.

A hanger is actually considered an offal, which is why it has a very deep and unique flavour. You need to be careful with it, though, because the longer you cook it, the tougher it gets.

It's not exactly a pretty steak – there's a sinew that runs down the middle (which your butcher can remove for you) that makes it a little irregular in shape. But who cares what it looks like when it tastes this good?

The best way to cook a hanger is on a high heat with a good long resting time. It also loves an overnight marinade, particularly one that includes some sort of citric acid, as this will break down any fibres and make it a little more tender.

As always, remove it from the fridge a few hours before cooking to bring to room temperature. Season the steak with good-quality sea salt when you take it out of the fridge.

Oil the steak just before cooking, then whack it on a really hot pan or barbecue until it reaches 48°C internally. Allow it to rest for at least 15 minutes before carving.

Reverse-seared rib of beef

Gaz says

When I first started talking about the reserve searing method, people went mad for it. It's probably the question that people ask me most on Twitter. So here's everything you need to know.

Basically, reverse searing means that you're cooking a steak backwards. Instead of searing in a hot pan then resting, you're flipping that method on its head.

You start by slow cooking your cut of beef in the oven at a very low heat until it reaches your desired temperature. Think of this more like the final burst of dry ageing – you're removing all the water from the beef and intensifying all the flavour.

When it's ready, it might look a bit grey and rubbery. But don't panic! This is where the sear comes in. You've already got a perfectly cooked bit of beef. All it needs now is a flash in a spanking hot pan or barbecue to caramelise the exterior and give it that banging char. You don't even need to rest it – the meat is already tender from the initial stage.

If you use a good digital meat probe thermometer and keep a close eye on the internal temperature, it's impossible to overcook. In fact, you can even leave it in an oven at 50°C and disappear for a few hours, knowing everything will be flawless when you return. Beef cooked this way is absolute perfection – a nice ruby red from edge to edge with a delicious char on the exterior.

I wouldn't attempt doing this with anything less than a steak for two that's 1 kilo with a bone (or 800g off the bone). It works really well with a 24oz rib-eye on the bone or côte de boeuf. The method on the next page is for a monster rib of beef, but really the method stays the same, no matter the cut.

There's no definitive cooking time for this. As a very rough guide, you need about an hour per kilo. But don't hold me to that – the most important thing is to keep a close eye on the internal temperature.

Which is why you absolutely need a digital meat probe thermometer. You leave this tucked horizontally into the meat while it's in the oven and keep a close eye on the rising temperature. The good news is that these are two a penny nowadays. You can pick them up anywhere for around €25. I use the Inkbird, but the Meatermade is also good.

Serves 6 (with enough left over for Barry's Dublin dip sandwiches)

1 x 3.5kg rib of beef, on the bone
Fine sea salt and freshly ground black pepper

Take your beef out of the fridge a few hours before cooking, season well with salt and pepper and bring it to room temperature.

Preheat the oven to 90°C (you can start at an even lower temperature if you have more time). Put the beef in a roasting tray, then insert your digital meat probe thermometer horizontally, letting the long cable trail out of the oven door (the cable should be thin enough to fit through the door). The aim here is to get the final temperature of the beef to 50°C, which is cooked rare.

Keep an eye on the increasing temperature of the beef. When it looks like it's approaching 35°C, keep an even closer eye on it as the temperature will start to increase more rapidly. You can even turn the oven down to 50°C at this stage.

When the beef is at 50°C internally, it's perfectly rare. So long as you're damn sure that your oven temperature is at an even 50°C (i.e. not reducing from 90°C), you can leave the beef in there for as long as you like. It simply cannot overcook.

When you're ready to eat, it's time to sear! Get that frying pan smoking hot (uh, maybe open a window or turn on the extractor fan) or get the barbecue piping hot. Whack the beef on, trying to get a good bit of colour all over the fat and the beef.

Again, you don't need to worry about resting it. Carve it up and mill into it.

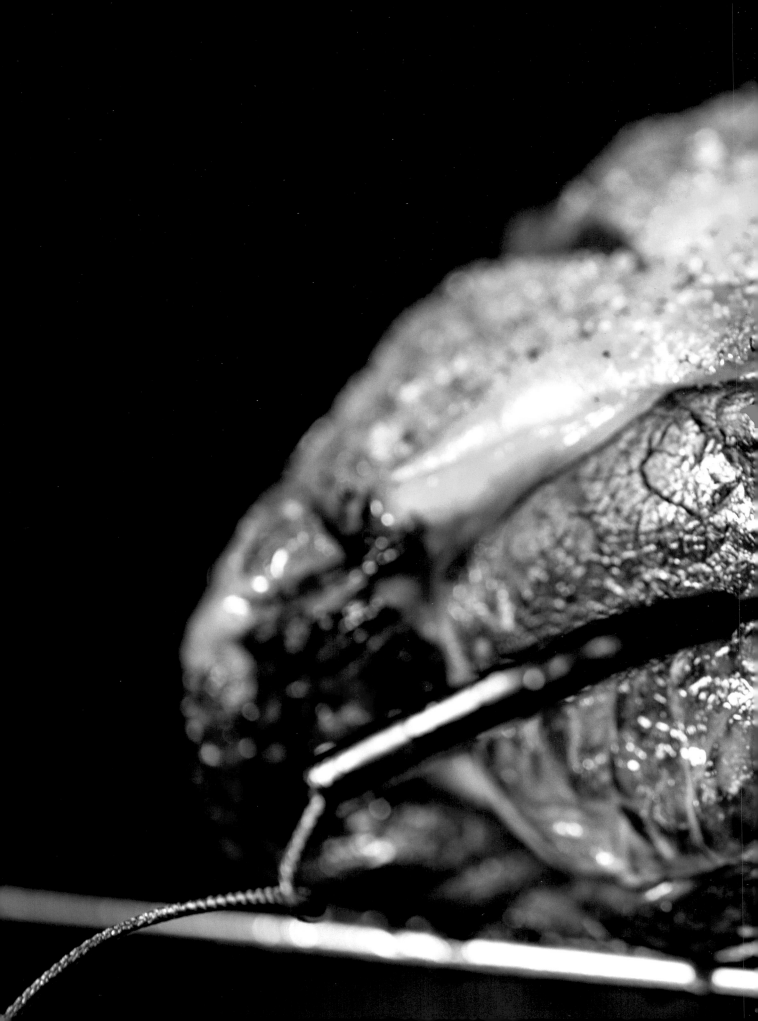

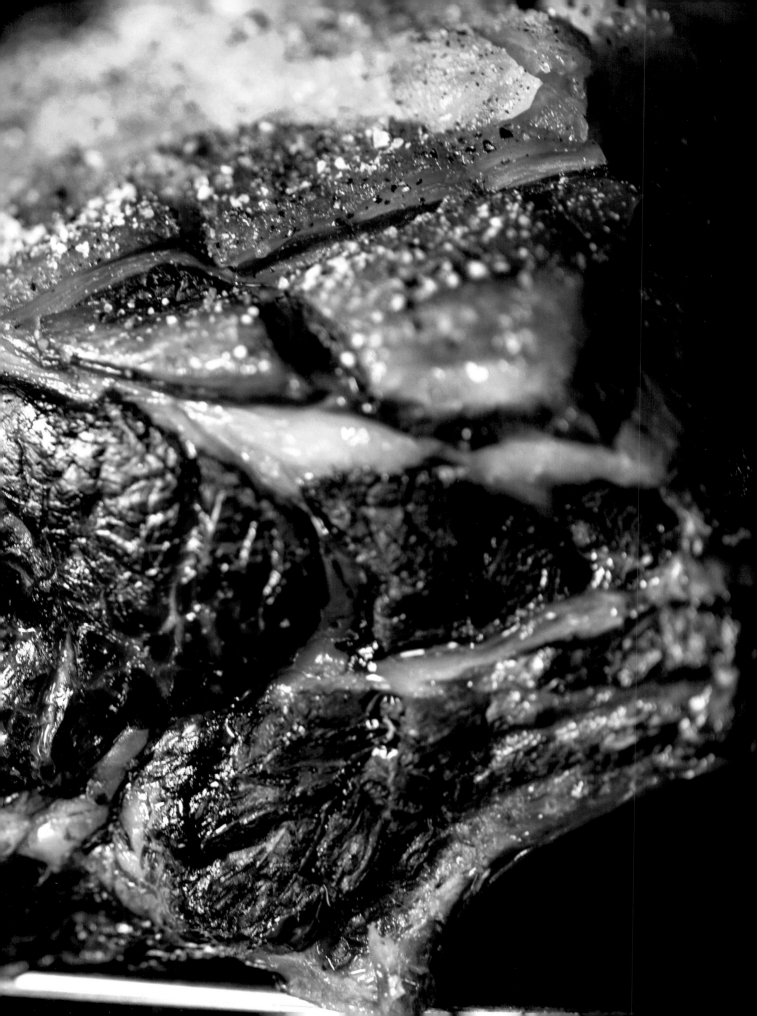

From farm to fork: The journey from the field to your plate.

Nicola Brady

I'll admit there are nicer places to spend a sunny afternoon than the inside of an abattoir. When you're in the door, there's no mistaking what is taking place. The floor is slick with blood and indistinguishable lumps of fat. To my right, the racks are lined up with the hearts and tongues of the cows, the hearts larger than an average chicken. To my left, the hide is being peeled off a cow as it hangs from four hooks.

But the feeling in the air is one of calm. The guys who are performing these tasks are doing so with a distinct sense of precision. Their knives are exacting and meticulous. Not a scrap of the animal is wasted. But more importantly, there's a huge feeling of respect for the animals. There is no sense of stress in the atmosphere, no feeling of anguish or upset. And that's exactly what you want when you're choosing where your meat comes from.

It's no accident that this is the case. Niall O'Gorman runs O'Gorman Meats with his brother, James, and their number one concern is the welfare of their animals.

'First of all, we don't want to be working in an area where there are stressed animals,' says Niall. 'That's the main thing. It's about our welfare as well – it's very, very dangerous. If you have a stressed-out animal down there, it's quite capable of killing you. We do everything in our power not to have it that way.'

If you think of a slaughterhouse, you might well imagine a factory-style conveyer belt where the cattle are fed through at ridiculous speeds. Make no mistake, those places do exist. They might be killing 3,000 cattle in one day, putting an animal through every 10 to 15 seconds. At O'Gorman, they process only 30 to 40 a day.

Which is why they can take the time to do their job properly. I was in the abattoir for a good four hours and at no time did I see or hear any sign of distress. That also comes down to the fact that the animals have a short journey to the slaughterhouse.

'Our big advantage here is the area we're in,' says Niall. 'Farmers don't want to be hauling cattle halfway across the country. They don't have the time and they don't want the expense.'

But it's not just about the hassle of a long drive. When cattle have only a short journey to make, the difference in their level of stress is huge. If you were to transport cattle all the way across the country, with them spending hours in the back of a truck, they panic. That stress causes weight loss as well as an increased risk when the animal arrives. Plus you'll often find multiple cattle transported together. They don't know each other and are all piled into the back of an arctic truck. It's a hugely stressful experience.

At a small family-run business like O'Gorman, it's a different story. 'Ninety-nine percent of our farmers are within a 10- or 15-mile radius of this abattoir. You'll see farmers coming in here with two or three cattle,' says Niall. 'Them cattle are after being reared together. There's no stress at all. As far as they know, they're being moved between fields or going into pens for feeding. So when they get into the pen at the back here, they just think they're going into winter feeding.'

When the animals arrive, they have no idea what's going on and, put frankly, they have no clue what's about to happen. They're calm and happy. From an ethical point of view, this is obviously of huge importance. But this also influences the flavour of the meat. 'Stress does affect the meat, there's no doubt about it,' says Rick. 'You can visually see how it affects the meat.'

There's another element at play here, which some abattoirs don't have the time for given the scale of their operation. At O'Gorman they use an electric stimulator that they clip to the ear when an animal is dead. This puts an electric current through the body that tenses all the muscles. When they then bleed the animal, the body totally relaxes and every drop of blood comes out. This leads to a far tastier product, but it's too time consuming for the bigger factories to bother with.

The other factor in the tasting process? Those green fields of Kildare. James O'Gorman lives just around the corner in a farmhouse overlooking the rolling hills of the thoroughbred county. There's something lovely about seeing the fields that the cows call home and knowing that they have all the space they desire to graze and roam.

I hopped the fence with Gaz (once we got permission from James, of course, along with a promise that there were no bulls in the field that would take a fancy to either one of us). There, we found a group of cattle living like a peaceful little family along with a chestnut horse who was either exceptionally friendly or protective of the young calves in the field. There was a herd of sheep hopping around, all of them living harmoniously with acres of land to enjoy.

While James is just a few minutes away, Niall is even closer – his farmhouse is right next to the abattoir itself. To say it's a family affair is an understatement. Their dad, Jim, still knocks around the place. The business has been in the family since 1960, when they started a little slaughterhouse at the back of an old butcher shop in Castledermot. There, they would kill maybe two or three cattle and a few lambs each week to butcher and sell in the shop. But a change in regulation and a demand for a bigger space saw them set up the abattoir in 1980. James and Niall have been involved since their teens.

Niall O'Gorman

James O'Gorman

'I'll never forget the first time I had to put a knife through the skin of an animal,' Niall tells me. 'I was 14 years of age and I'll remember it until the day I die. It's the hardest thing I ever had to do. My father was standing over me and he just kept saying, "Take your time." At 14 years of age, it's an extremely hard thing to do.'

It's clear from talking to Niall that slaughtering isn't something he takes lightly. There's no cavalier attitude to it. He respects the animals, the farmers and the process. He's exactly the kind of man you want to do the job.

'You get used to it over the years. You don't mind it as much. But that comes from knowing we're treating the cattle with respect.'

This is where the journey begins, but there's a way to go before the beef ends up on the plate. It's relationships like the one he has with Rick that show how important the line of respect is between the farmer, the slaughterman and the butcher.

Back in the day Niall worked with Rick's dad when he ran Higgins Family Butcher. It's those relationships, built up over decades, that are absolutely crucial.

It also means that Niall knows exactly what his customers are after and can tell immediately who will want which cow. 'You saw where I was down there on the slaughtering floor. I'm watching them carcasses coming down the line and I have a customer picked out for each one in my head. Before that animal goes around me, I'm looking at it and thinking "That'll suit so-and-so, that'll suit Rick" because every butcher is different.'

Even before Gaz spots a Dexter that would be perfect for the restaurant, Niall has earmarked it for him and Rick, knowing that this carcass would be their idea of absolute perfection. 'Before I even saw they were Dexters I knew I wanted those animals,' Gaz says to Niall. 'I saw them straight away. Even before you'd pointed them out to me, I'd taken a photo and knew I wanted one. It was exactly our type. And you knew it too.'

What made it perfect? The somewhat bronzed colour of the thick fat cap, its slight transparency and the colour of the ribs. Without knowing it, the slaughterman, butcher and chef had all selected the same heifer, knowing it was destined to end up on a platter in Michael's, slathered in garlic butter.

It's that kind of skill, knowledge and instinct that are incredibly hard to teach, and which are becoming all the more rare.

'I'll never forget the first time I had to put a knife through the skin of an animal. I was 14 years of age and I'll remember it until the day I die. It's the hardest thing I ever had to do. My father was standing over me and he just kept saying, "Take your time." At 14 years of age, it's an extremely hard thing to do.'

Niall O'Gorman

'I'm blessed that I got the training I did get. If it wasn't for my dad, I wouldn't be able to do what I do. Most kids coming up will never get that training again. I remember being brought into my uncle's shop when I was seven years of age. We'd be off school and were brought in to clean the machines. Basically minding us in the shop. I liked it; my sisters hated it.'

Rick Higgins

'There's butchers out there now, especially young lads, and they're trained in the supermarkets,' says Niall. 'They can look all they like at what's coming in that door, but they won't have a clue. They won't know whether that's a heifer or a steer, whether it's 90 years old or two years old. The old butchers, with Rick's training, they're brought up to recognise the good animals. The ones with the marbling, the nice heifer, the nice Angus. They know it.'

Rick agrees. 'I'm blessed that I got the training I did get,' he says. 'If it wasn't for my dad, I wouldn't be able to do what I do. Most kids coming up will never get that training again. I remember being brought into my uncle's shop when I was seven years of age. We'd be off school and were brought in to clean the machines. Basically minding us in the shop. I liked it; my sisters hated it.'

While Gaz and Rick have years, not decades, behind them in their working relationship, they still have a level of trust and understanding, even if it's hidden beneath slagging and endless bartering. 'I know exactly what Gaz will want,' says Rick. 'Generally, customers are coming to me because they like the way I age the beef and they like the way I do the fat and marbling. Gaz gets first selection – he gets treated like a fucking baby!'

That relationship and sense of trust goes right down the line from the farmer to the chef. Niall gets a call from the farmer and knows exactly what he has. He knows that if he gets a fat animal through the door, he'll be giving Rick a call. And Rick knows that Gaz will go bananas for a cow with a nice thick fat cap on it.

The farmers even come in to help with the slaughtering and the lads in the slaughterhouse go out and help in the fields too. 'Farmers are the most loyal men in the world, if you can stay in with them,' says Niall.

But it seems to me like the loyalty works in every direction. The farmer needs to trust that they're taking their cattle to a slaughterhouse where they'll be treated with respect. After all, they've cared for these animals for years and nurtured them. In turn, the slaughterhouse needs to know that the carcasses they send out to butchers will be treated properly, aged in a way that will maximise their flavour and appreciated for what they are. And, of course, the chef needs to trust that the butcher will give them the best meat for their restaurant. It goes all the way down the chain.

I've always believed that if you're going to eat meat, you should know the reality of where it comes from. There's nothing comfortable about the killing floor. There's sure as hell nothing glamorous about it. But pretending that the cow leaps straight from the field onto your plate doesn't do anyone any favours.

Knowing that an animal has been cared for at every step of the way, treated with respect and slaughtered in an ethical way is a source of comfort. When you sit down to enjoy an epic picanha steak or a juicy rib-eye with a nice crisp fat cap, you want to be safe in the knowledge that the cow on your plate lived a good life and was treated well.

And when this is the place that your steak comes from, you can be damn sure that's the case.

One-pot wonders.

One-hour roast chicken 161

Chicken, turnip and barley stew 162

Jungle curry (that isn't) 164

Dirty 'fried' rice with sesame, chilli and ginger 167

One-hour roast chicken

6 medium Rooster potatoes, peeled and halved lengthways
4 medium carrots, peeled, topped and tailed, and cut lengthways
2 medium brown onions, quartered
¼ turnip (roughly 200g), peeled and cut into 12 pieces
8 garlic cloves, unpeeled and left whole
6–7 sprigs of fresh thyme
125ml vegetable oil
1 x 1.5–1.7kg whole chicken
Fine sea salt and freshly ground black pepper

To serve
Chicken wing gravy (page 227)

Preheat the oven to 200°C.

Place all the veg, garlic and thyme sprigs in the base of a large baking tray with a small lip (you don't want a high-sided roasting tin because the chicken will steam in it and we want it to crisp up). Put the veg that you want to get a bit crisp (like the potatoes) around the edges of the tray and the veg that you want to soak up the chicken juices in the middle of the tray. The carrots work really well right under the chicken. Drizzle them all generously with the oil.

Pop the chicken right on top of the veg in the middle of the tray and rub the oil all over the chicken, then season really well with salt and pepper. The key here is to liberally cover absolutely everything with oil, otherwise you're dry roasting. And that's shite.

Roast in the oven for 15 minutes, then crack open the oven door for a few seconds to release that first puff of steam – this will help you get crisp skin. Continue to roast for another 20 minutes, then take the tray out and baste the chicken and veg will all the delicious pan juices. You can give the veg a bit of a gentle stir around if you like.

Return to the oven, turning the tray around as you do. Most ovens cook faster at the back, so this will give your chicken an even cook. Roast for another 15 minutes.

Remove the roasted chicken from the tray and put it on a rack to rest while you continue to cook the veg in the oven for the final 10 minutes.

Carve the chicken and serve with the roasted veg and our chicken wing gravy.

Gaz says
Who doesn'tlove a roast chicken? I'd often just chuck one into the oven without a plan and then horse into the whole thing myself like I'm Henry VIII. Actually, a friend once nicknamed me Henry VIII after she walked in and caught me eating a whole roast duck all by myself. I regret nothing.

One time I went to the deli counter when I was badly hungover. I bought a full baguette, a rotisserie chicken and a tub of coleslaw. Soon I realised that I'd eaten so much of it that the only solution was to finish the whole lot, hide all the evidence and pretend that the whole sordid thing had never happened. An hour later, Rita landed home with a roast chicken from the same deli counter. And I ate it. That's the story of my life.

Anyway, I suppose you can always roast a chicken and share it with other people, like some kind of weirdo, and this is the easiest way in the world to do it. You fuck everything in the pan and all the gorgeous fat and juices from the chicken drip all over the vegetables and turn it into a pan of lusciousness. If you want the spuds a little crispier, leave them on the outside but put the onions and carrots right under the chicken.

Five minutes of prep, an hour or so in the oven and you're sorted. And if you do end up eating the whole lot by yourself, just be sure to hide the carcass right at the bottom of the bin. I won't tell a soul.

Chef's tip
You mightn't believe that you can cook a chicken in an hour, but you absolutely can. This was tested in a regular home oven and came out perfectly. However, if you've got a bigger chicken or have a shit oven, you can always cook it for a few minutes longer. I won't mind.

Serves 4

Chicken, turnip and barley stew

Gaz says

This is my go-to dish when I feel a bit muggy and have had a load of crazy days in a row. I always crave it when I feel a bit tired and 'off' in general. When I eat this stew, I just feel good – it's comfort food in its purest form. More importantly, I also feel great the next day because it's so easy to digest and barley is so soothing. The temptation when you're knackered is to order a takeaway or go to the chipper, but you can be left feeling like shit the next morning. With this stew, you feel great. It's my little secret weapon.

And it's so easy to make too. I chuck everything in the pressure cooker at home and it cooks in no time. By the time I have a shower and get back downstairs in my Nigella-esque silk pyjamas, it's done and ready.

Chef's tip

Because I use a pressure cooker, I don't bother browning anything off. If you're going to use a pressure cooker too, you can skip the entire method and just chuck in the whole lot, following the instructions on the cooker. It's the easiest dinner in the world.

Serves 4

Vegetable oil
1.5kg free-range chicken thighs
3 small brown onions, diced
3 small carrots, peeled and diced
3 celery sticks, diced
3 large Rooster potatoes, peeled and diced
½ small turnip, peeled and diced
3 garlic cloves, finely chopped
Fine sea salt and freshly ground black pepper
1.5 litres chicken stock
1 large leek, sliced into 2mm-thick rings
150g pearl barley
4–5 sprigs of fresh thyme
A large handful of fresh curly parsley, finely chopped

Place a very large pot over a high heat along with a good glug of oil.

Add your chicken thighs in batches and brown them off, making sure you get a gorgeous brown crust on each piece. As each thigh crisps up, remove it from the pot and rest them on a baking tray. Continue cooking until all your thighs are brown.

To the same pot (which now has lovely crisp chicken bits on its bottom), add your onions, carrots, celery, potatoes, turnip and garlic along with three good pinches of salt. Turn down the heat to medium to sweat off all the veg for 10–15 minutes.

Add your stock and give it all a good stir, then add your browned chicken thighs back to the pot and simmer for 25 minutes.

After 25 minutes, add the leek and barley. Give the whole lot another really good stir and simmer for another 30 minutes, until the leek and barley are cooked. Season to taste with salt and pepper.

Right at the end, add the leaves from the thyme stalks and most of the chopped curly parsley, holding some back for serving.

This is best served warm rather than hot. Leave it for half an hour and all those flavours will just relax into each other. Sprinkle the last bits of chopped parsley on top right before serving.

Slurp it down and try to remember that everything will be okay.

Jungle curry (that isn't)

Gaz says

To be honest, I don't even think we can call this a jungle curry. A jungle curry doesn't have coconut milk or dairy and this one, um, does. The problem I had is that my version without coconut wasn't very good. I wasn't happy with the background spices, but as soon as I added in a bit of coconut milk, it was amazing. It just brought everything together.

Chef's tip

Whenever I do a curry at home, I make it in the morning, then pick up all the naan, rice, poppadoms and so on from the Indian takeaway on the way home. It's still a nice homemade dinner, but your life is made that little bit easier.

Serves 4

4 tablespoons sunflower oil
600kg pork belly meat, cut into 2.5–5cm cubes
2 aubergines, skin removed and cut into chunks
2 heaped tablespoons Mae Ploy red curry paste
50g garlic, minced
30g fresh ginger, peeled and minced
4 star anise
1 tablespoon coriander seeds
1 x 400g tin of chopped tomatoes
50g golden raisins or sultanas
1 litre beef stock
200ml coconut milk
3 dried lime leaves
1 tablespoon tamarind paste
Fine sea salt

To serve
Boiled basmati rice (or see the chef's tip)

Add the oil to a large non-stick pan or pot over a medium-high heat. Add the cubes of pork and fry for 5–6 minutes, then add the aubergines and fry until the aubergines are light golden brown.

Spoon in the red curry paste and allow it to sweat in the pan. The key here is to keep it moving – try to spread it evenly around the entirety of the pan. The more of the base of the pan is covered with the paste, the tastier it will be.

Add your garlic, ginger, star anise and coriander seeds and combine well. After 2–3 minutes, once the spices have all sweated down and are working through the veg and pork, add your tinned tomatoes, then the raisins or sultanas, followed by the beef stock. Simmer for 5 minutes before adding the coconut milk, lime leaves and tamarind paste. Cover with a lid and gently simmer for 3 hours. Season with salt to taste.

Serve with boiled basmati rice.

Dirty 'fried' rice with sesame, chilli and ginger

400g basmati rice

4 garlic cloves, roughly chopped

1 x 2cm cube of fresh ginger, peeled and minced

500ml chicken stock

1 star anise

2 pinches of chilli flakes

A pinch of coriander seeds

1 teaspoon butter

A small pinch of fine sea salt

Whatever leftover meat and/or vegetables you have (see the chef's tip)

2 spring onions, finely chopped

150ml Asian dressing (page 234)

2 glugs of sesame oil

2 tablespoons vegetable oil, for frying (optional)

1 egg yolk

Soak the rice in a bowl of water for 20 minutes, then rinse it two or three times until the water runs clear and there is no cloudiness coming out of it at all. The aim is to get rid of all the starch.

Add the rice to a rice cooker along with the garlic, ginger, stock, star anise, chilli flakes, coriander seeds, butter and salt. If you're including some leftover meat or veg in your dish, now is the time to chuck that in too. The rice cooker will warm it through.

Cook the rice for 15–20 minutes. Remove and allow to cool thoroughly before stirring in the spring onions, Asian dressing and sesame oil. You can either eat it right now or you can fry it up in a pan.

To fry it, heat 2 tablespoons of oil in a large frying pan over a medium heat, then add the rice and spread it all out in the pan. Let the rice fry off without touching it – that way, you'll get a nice crisp crust on the bottom.

Whichever way you're eating the finished product, turn it out into a large serving bowl and serve immediately with a raw egg yolk on top. Just before eating, pierce the yolk and swirl all its yellowy goodness throughout the rice.

Gaz says

This is another one of my go-to dishes to make at home. And out of all the (many) kitchen gadgets I've got knocking around, the rice cooker has proved to be the best value. They cost about €30 and you get perfectly cooked rice every single time.

If you flavour the stock well, your rice will always be banging. I always put a bit of oil and butter in too because … well, have we met?! Technically this isn't a fried rice, but it has all the same flavour with far less dicking around. I personally love to eat it straight from the rice cooker. If you want to whack it in a frying pan at the end, though, work away.

Chef's tip

This recipe gives you a good solid base for whatever else you want to chuck in. In my fridge, there are always some scraps of a leftover joint lying around. Whatever meat you have knocking about, throw it in. I always chuck in whatever veg I have lying around too. In my house, this dish is never the same twice.

Serves 4

Sandwiches and burgers.

Crisp sandwich   173
Fried Gruyère and honey sandwich   174
Smash burger   176
Barry's Dublin dip   179

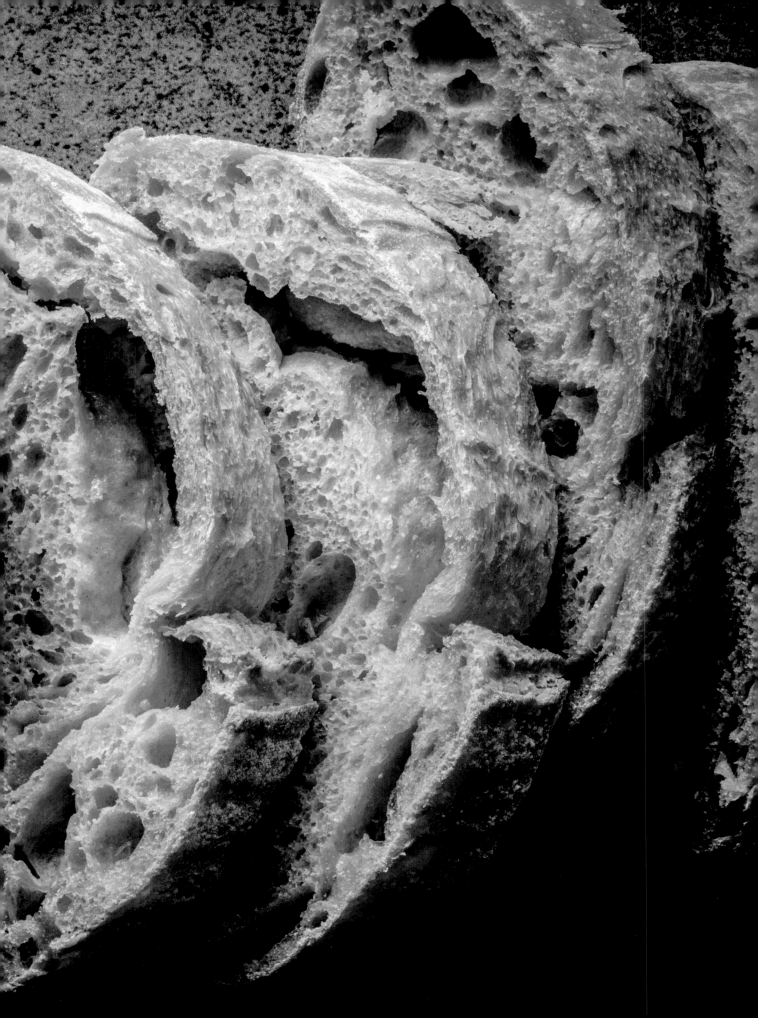

Crisp sandwich

Gaz says
I henceforth decree my rules for the perfect crisp sambo:

1. The only acceptable bread to use is shitty, plasticky sliced pan.

2. The crisp sambo must never include ham or cheese. This is dining in its purest form.

3. You have to use butter and it has to be Kerrygold. If you use margarine, you're barred from Michael's for life.

Makes 1

2 slices of shitty white bread
Very soft butter, preferably Kerrygold
1 bag of crisps, preferably Tayto but always cheese and onion, end of story

Generously slather your shitty white bread with twice the amount of butter you think you need. The butter has to be ladled on so thick that you leave teeth marks with every bite.

Slightly crunch the bag of crisps. Carefully pour the crisps onto the buttered bottom slice of bread. Put the other slice of bread on top ever so gently, then smash it all down with your meaty paw so hard that you leave a hand imprint in the bread.

Eat it with no plate so the crisps fall out and all over your chest. Alternatively, eat while standing over the sink, like a racoon eating over a dustbin.

Fried Gruyère and honey sandwich

Gaz says

Do you remember back in the 1980s when it was so trendy to have deep-fried Brie on the menu? That's kind of been lost, but to me, it's a dish that never should have been phased out. Fried cheese in breadcrumbs – what's not to like? It's been on both our menus for ages. We use Brie in Michael's and Gruyère in Little Mike's. Both dishes absolutely fly out the door. It's what the people want!

I would often bring some breadcrumbed cheese home, fry it up and shove it in a sandwich. Fried shit in bread will always, always be a good idea. This, to me, belongs in a white roll with a good crusty exterior with cloudlike, fluffy insides filled with hot cheese, honey and butter. You can't argue with that.

Seriously. Try me. You'll lose.

Makes 2

50g plain flour
2 eggs, beaten
50g panko breadcrumbs
250g Gruyère cheese, cut into 2.5cm fingers
Sunflower oil, for deep-frying
2 crusty bread rolls, buttered
A good drizzle of honey
Crispy fried onions (optional)

Make three little bowls for your breadcrumbing station: one with the flour, one with the beaten eggs and one with the breadcrumbs.

First pop your Gruyère cheese fingers in the flour, then dunk them in the eggs before finally giving them a good covering of the breadcrumbs. Make sure you press the breadcrumbs in and ensure that every little bit is covered. Set them aside.

You can cook these either in a deep-fryer or in a frying pan. At 180°C, they will take roughly 4–5 minutes. You want them nice and golden, but not overcooked – you want to bite into the cheese and get a bit of a goo going, but you don't want it to burst in the fryer. Don't forget, the cheese will continue to cook and melt a little when it's resting, so err on the side of caution.

To serve, wedge the golden cheese into a buttered crusty roll, giving it a good drizzle of honey when it's warm and tucked up into its little bread bed.

I always have a bag of crispy fried onions knocking around the kitchen, so I like to give this a little sprinkle of those for a bit of extra flavour and crunch. But that's just me. I've also had great success adding in a few very thin slices of red onion, but if you've got neither, don't worry – your sandwich will still be fucking paradise.

Smash burger

Gaz says

When I make a burger, 90% of the time it's a smash burger. They cook quickly and they're perfect every time. It's a one-pan wonder. I like my burger patties to be a bit fattier because … well, have you met me? I'm a goddamned greasehound and proud of it.

What's great about this burger is how all the elements merge and mingle together in the pan, like they're dancing some kind of sexy tango. You're left with a perfectly cooked, slightly charred patty, gooey cheese and a bun that yields to the steam until it's as soft as a pillow. In fact, sometimes I even wrap this up in foil for a few minutes so that when I open it up it's even steamier. Heaven.

And yeah, yeah, I know it's cheap plasticky cheese, but it works perfectly in burgers. Don't @ me.

Makes 2

2 brioche burger buns
2 tablespoons piquant burger sauce (page 233)
A drizzle of ketchup
A drizzle of yellow American mustard
4 slices of gherkins
300g beef mince with a 30% fat ratio, coarsely ground
A splash of vegetable oil
Fine sea salt and freshly ground black pepper
1 small onion, very thinly sliced (halved or rings)
4 Easi-singles
2 swigs of beer

Start by dressing your burger buns with the piquant burger sauce, ketchup, mustard and gherkins. You need to dress them now because you have to work quickly at the end.

Heat a frying pan on a high heat until it's smoking. While that's heating up, make four meatballs with roughly 75g beef each. Don't pack them tightly, as their looseness allows the delicious fat to render into all the little pockets in the burger.

Unless you've got a monster frying pan, you'll probably be cooking these two at a time. Throw a splash of oil into the pan, then add the meatballs. Being really careful of splashing hot oil, place a piece of parchment paper on top of the meatballs, then smash them down into burgers using the base of another heavy pan. You want to smash them down so they're as thin as possible.

Remove the parchment paper, then season the burgers with salt and pepper and add a few thin slices of onion on each burger. Cook for 3–4 minutes, until they're about 70% cooked on one side. Flip them over and cook for 1 minute more to finish cooking the burger and to gently fry the onions.

Take the pan off the heat and assemble the burger in the pan. Each burger gets a dressed bun, two patties and two slices of cheese.

Once assembled, throw in a swig of beer and cover the pan (with the burger still in the pan). Leave it covered for 1 minute, until the bun is warm and the cheese has melted in the residual heat and steam.

Repeat the process with the other burger and waste no time smashing it into your gob.

Barry's Dublin dip

1 red onion, unpeeled and cut in half lengthways
1 tablespoon olive oil
1 tablespoon balsamic vinegar
1 teaspoon honey
2 thick slices of granary or sourdough bread
100g reverse-seared beef (see page 136), chilled and thinly sliced
50g grated Dubliner or Cheddar cheese

For the tarragon mayo
A big pinch of finely chopped fresh tarragon leaves
1 tablespoon mayonnaise
½ teaspoon Dijon mustard
Fine sea salt and freshly ground black pepper

For dipping
60ml chicken wing gravy (page 227)

Preheat the oven to 180°C.

Place your red onion cut side down in a hot, dry ovenproof frying pan over a high heat, then drizzle over the olive oil. After 2 minutes, turn down the heat to medium and add the balsamic vinegar and honey, giving it all a swoosh around. Cook in the pan until the onion is caramelised, then turn it over so that the cut side is now facing up and transfer the pan to the oven to cook for 20 minutes.

Mix the tarragon with the mayo and mustard and season with salt and pepper. You can blend this with a stick blender if you like if you're making a big batch.

To assemble, lightly toast the bread, then smear it generously with the mayo. Pile the beef and grated cheese onto the bottom slice.

Take the onion out of the oven and carefully squeeze the flesh from the skin. Put that onion onto the cheese, then top with the other slice of bread. Put it back in the frying pan and back in the oven to cook for 5–7 minutes, until the cheese has melted.

Serve with the little pot of chicken wing gravy, dunking in each bite before you eat. Heaven.

Barry says
In 147 Deli we do a different special each week and the Dublin dip is one that has an army of loyal fans. It's essentially a French dip sandwich with reverse-seared topside beef, melted cheese and a really good, rich chicken stock for dipping. The first one we made used Dubliner cheese, so that's how it got the name. We always mix it up, though.

That's why I do the specials in 147. It keeps me sane. If I were to do the same sandwich every week, I'd go bananas. It allows me to have a bit of fun in the kitchen and get creative.

Chef's tip
Make sure the beef is sliced thin and chopped up in the sandwich. You don't want to be pulling half the meat out in one mouthful. Chilling it overnight helps to get those thin slices.

Makes 1

Salads and sides.

Black pudding strudel   185
Mushroom and mozzarella arancini   186
60:40 mash   191
Barry's Asian-style slaw   192
Asian noodle salad   195
Rita's rice salad   197
Fennel, orange and grape salad   198
Cabbage, garlic and caraway salad   201
Sneaky sauerkraut   203

Black pudding strudel

3 sheets of filo pastry, roughly A4 size, thawed
60g butter, melted
A handful of panko breadcrumbs
250g soft black pudding (a boudin noir or Inch House pudding;
see the chef's tip)
A splash of cream (optional)
1 teaspoon roughly chopped fresh flat-leaf parsley
3 tablespoons apple chutney (page 238 or shop-bought) or
shop-bought red onion marmalade

Preheat the oven to 200°C. Line a baking sheet with non-stick baking paper.

Lay the first sheet of filo down flat on a clean, damp tea towel. Brush the sheet liberally with melted butter and a scattering of breadcrumbs. Put the second sheet of filo next to the first one so that the two shorter ends are overlapping a bit, almost like you're making one long sheet of filo pastry, and give that one a buttery brush and the breadcrumb scatter too. Put the third sheet of filo on top of the other two where they're overlapping to reinforce the middle.

Crumble the pudding into a bowl and add a splash of cream if necessary to get it to the consistency of raw sausage meat.

Put the pudding in a line at the bottom of the long side of the sheet, about four-fifths of the way down. Leave a border that's 4–5cm clear at the bottom of the pastry and to the left and right of the pudding.

Sprinkle the pudding with your parsley, then add the apple chutney or red onion marmalade on top. Spread it out as best you can.

What you're basically doing now is rolling up a big jam roly-poly … of sorts. Give your hands a wash because you want the pastry to be rolled very cleanly and you are most likely a filthy dirt bird. Fold the bottom line of the pastry over the pudding, then roll it all up like a meaty roly-poly.

You should have about a 3cm border to either side of the pudding parcel. Trim these down if they're bigger, then fold them over the pudding section. Transfer to the lined baking tray, seam side down.

Brush generously with more melted butter and bake in the oven for 12–15 minutes, until it's golden brown and crisp.

Gaz says

Right. There may have been a bit of a debate about whether or not this is an acceptable side dish. But I suppose calling this a side dish is in keeping with my stance on food in general. In my eyes, black pudding can legitimately be classified as a side vegetable. It's basically a salad.

But whatever you call it, it's bloody gorgeous (no pun intended). It's crisp, it's unctuous inside, there's a bit of fruitiness … it's kind of like a jazzed-up sausage roll. Put this on the side of any roast meat and trust me, your guests will think you're a goddamned genius.

Chef's tip

Most black pudding that you find in the shops is quite stiff. If you can't find a boudin noir (which is a little looser), then mix your pudding with a splash of cream to get a more malleable texture.

Serves 2–4

Mushroom and mozzarella arancini

Gaz says

We always have loads of arancini on the go in the restaurant and we always sneak a few onto our platters as well. The key is to really pack the stock you cook the rice in with heaps of flavour. The rice is going to soak up every last little drop, so you want to make it as tasty as you possibly can. Feel free to get creative with these too. We make loads of different varieties in the restaurant, like wild duck and mushroom or our favourite Lambay Island crab. Basically, you can chuck anything you like in there. But the key is sneaking a little bit of cheese right into the middle of each arancini ball so that you're met with a gooey cheese surprise when you bite in.

Serves 4

2 knobs of butter
Vegetable oil, for deep-frying
100g chestnut mushrooms, finely chopped
100g wild mushrooms, finely chopped
2 shallots, thinly sliced
1 garlic clove, finely chopped
250g Carnaroli rice
A glass of white wine (plus a glass for the chef)
Fine sea salt and freshly ground black pepper
A handful of grated mozzarella
A big handful of baby spinach, finely chopped
4 big pinches of fresh tarragon leaves
A good pinch of chopped fresh flat-leaf parsley
1 ball of buffalo mozzarella, cut into 1cm pieces

For the mushroom stock
100g dried mushrooms
1.2 litres beef or chicken stock

For the coating
60g plain flour
3 eggs, beaten
100g breadcrumbs (panko are the best for a crisp finish)

Recipe overleaf >

First off, make your mushroom stock. Gently heat the dried mushrooms and your beef stock in a small saucepan for 15 minutes to release all the flavours. Blitz it up with a stick blender, then increase the heat to high and reduce until you've got roughly 300ml of mushroom stock. Keep it hot on a low heat on the hob.

Meanwhile, melt a knob of butter and a splash of oil in a frying pan. Add your chestnut and wild mushrooms and give them a good sear on a high heat. Allow them to wilt down and release their moisture, but don't stop there – keep cooking until the moisture has been reabsorbed by the mushrooms. Mushrooms are mostly water and water tastes of nothing, so cooking them this way pumps them up with flavour. Remove the pan from the heat and leave to one side.

Next up, make your rice. Only do this when you have about 15 minutes ahead of you with no distractions. You're basically making a risotto here. This can be done a few hours ahead, as you need to leave the rice to cool before you form the arancini balls anyway.

In a large heavy-based saucepan or casserole set over a low to medium heat, sweat off the shallots and garlic in a good knob of butter. You want them softened but not coloured. Add the rice and cook the whole lot gently for a few minutes to get a bit of nuttiness in the pan. If anything starts to colour, turn the heat down.

Now throw in your glass of wine. And make sure your own glass is close to hand because you're not going to leave the stovetop any time soon. Grab your wooden spoon and start stirring the risotto. Do. Not. Stop. Even if the house is on fire around you, do not stop stirring that bloody risotto. The risotto succeeds or fails on the stirring – the more you stir, the better the end result.

Add the hot mushroom stock one ladleful at a time, still stirring all the time. Only add more when the previous ladle has been gobbled up by the rice. All in all, this should take 10–12 minutes, until the rice is just undercooked and nicely holding together. Add the sautéed mushrooms.

Check the seasoning, adding salt and pepper to taste. Once you're happy, add the grated mozzarella and stir to combine, then add the spinach, tarragon and parsley.

Pour the whole lot into a wide, shallow tray, spreading it out evenly. Let it cool down, then pop it in the fridge, covered tightly, until you're ready to form the arancini balls.

Get the chilled arancini mix out of the fridge and roll it into little balls the size of ping pong balls. You should get around 16 balls from the mixture. When you've got the rough shape, flatten it out a little in your palm and poke a small piece of the buffalo mozzarella in the middle. Shape the rest of the ball around that little piece of cheese, making sure it's completely tucked into the middle.

Get three wide, shallow bowls set up: one with the flour, one with the beaten eggs and one with the breadcrumbs.

Dip your arancini balls in the flour, then the beaten eggs, then the breadcrumbs. Make sure they're well coated in the breadcrumbs.

If you're using a deep-fryer, heat the oil to 180°C and deep-fry in batches until golden brown. Remember, everything in the middle is cooked already – you just want to heat the mixture and melt the cheese inside. If you're pan-frying them in oil, don't be afraid to squish them down a little to make your life easier. Drain on kitchen paper for a minute or two before burning your mouth on them because you couldn't wait a moment longer to eat them.

60:40 mash

950g peeled Rooster potatoes
570g butter
A splash of milk
A generous pinch of fine sea salt

This is an easy one. Simply steam the whole peeled potatoes until a skewer goes through them easily. They should be slightly floury on the outside and ever so slightly firm on the inside.

Heat up the butter and milk in a small saucepan just until the butter has melted, then add to the hot potatoes. Never throw cold butter or milk into your mash or it will end up lumpy. The potatoes should be hot, the milk should be warm and the butter should be melted.

Mash it all with a masher and a generous pinch of salt. This step is all the more important because you've steamed the spuds rather than boiled them in salty water, so don't be stingy.

Finish them off with a whisk if you want to get jazzy (see the chef's tip). Eat with a spoon and a massive smile on your face.

Gaz says
60% potatoes. 40% butter. 100% deliciousness.

There's no secret as to why this is so damn good. When you're dealing with that amount of butter, how can anything be wrong? Forget about the lumpy mash your granny used to make. This stuff glistens like silk and pours like a mousse. It's just heaven. Don't tell anyone, but I actually make 50:50 mash. But that's obscene.

I first had mash like this in Sheen Falls, years ago. I always thought my mash was good, but this was just next level. And each time I make it now, I'm transported right back to that day and the very first moment I ate it, just like that scene in *Ratatouille*.

Oh, and by the way, I know that the splash of milk actually makes this more of a 59:39:2 mash. But this isn't a maths book, so leave me alone.

Chef's tip
Once you've mashed the potatoes, give them a bit of a whip with a whisk. That way, you'll get an extra creamy mash.

Serves 4

Barry's Asian-style slaw

Barry says

I think about food pretty much 24/7. There are always ideas knocking around in my head. If I'm sitting idle and a notion springs into my head, I'll always give it a go. And this is one of those ideas that really works.

This goes with so many things, but it works really well with chicken and pork. If you want a fresh, crunchy slaw that has a bit of bite, mix it all together 10 minutes before you're eating. But if you want more of a folding slaw, which will yield softly into a sandwich, you can make it the day before.

I make this all the time and it changes a little bit each time, so don't be afraid to experiment. All the sauces used here can be found in any good Asian supermarket.

Serves 4

1 small head of red cabbage, finely shredded
½ head of white cabbage, finely shredded
2 carrots, peeled and grated
1 bunch of fresh coriander, chopped

For the dressing
2 garlic cloves, minced
150ml rice wine vinegar
50ml toasted sesame oil
1 tablespoon gochujang chilli paste
1 tablespoon LGM peanuts in chilli oil (or any other chilli oil)
1 tablespoon Kewpie mayo

To serve
1 bunch of spring onions, thinly sliced
1 small bag of salted peanuts, chopped

First off, whisk together all the dressing ingredients until you have a nice smooth paste.

Put the cabbage, carrots and coriander in a large bowl and mix with your hands to combine them well. Toss through the dressing, ensuring everything gets a nice covering. Finally, throw the spring onions and salted peanuts on top.

Asian noodle salad

This is a proper showstopper of a side dish. In fact, it's one of those sides that can easily outshine the mains. It's the perfect dish to have at a barbecue – it complements the smokiness of the meat really well, but also has enough flavour of its own to have a bit of personality. It's slippery, packed with flavour and you get a nice bit of crunch and saltiness from the peanuts too.

It's better made a few hours ahead so that you can let the dressing really permeate the noodles. But once you've made it, leave it to sit at room temperature – if you chill noodles, they're never the same. If you want to, you could also eat this as a main dish and serve it warm with a bit of chicken thrown in.

Serves 2

340g medium egg noodles
4 tablespoons runny honey
250ml Asian dressing (page 234)
A handful of fresh coriander, finely chopped
125g unsalted peanuts, finely chopped

Cook your noodles according to the packet instructions, minus 1 minute. You want them to be soft but not fully cooked. I often just leave them to soak in a Pyrex bowl covered in cling film. When you're happy, drain the noodles and put them into a large bowl.

Whisk the honey into the Asian dressing, then slather it all on top of the noodles and toss well to combine.

Serve with the chopped coriander and peanuts sprinkled on top.

Rita's rice salad

200g basmati rice
4 garlic cloves, roughly chopped
1 teaspoon butter
600ml chicken stock
A big pinch of fine sea salt
2 red onions, very finely diced
3 spring onions, chopped
½ cucumber, peeled, deseeded and finely diced
175g cooked ham, finely chopped
100g tinned baby peas, drained
100g tinned sweetcorn (if you like), drained
80g gherkins, chopped
3–4 tablespoons mayo
2 tablespoons white wine vinegar
2 tablespoons horseradish cream
A large handful of fresh flat-leaf parsley, very finely chopped

Soak the rice in cold water for 20 minutes, then drain and rinse it two or three times, until the water runs completely clear.

Add to a rice cooker along with the garlic, butter and stock as well as a big pinch of salt. Cook the rice for 15–20 minutes, until tender. Remove and allow to cool.

To make the salad, combine all the remaining ingredients with the cooled rice. You want to add only enough mayo to lightly bind the salad together, so add 3 tablespoons to start and only add more if you think it needs it. You don't want a big sloppy mess of mayo.

Transfer to a large serving bowl and put it on the table, ready to be met with rapturous applause.

Gaz says

Rita makes this as a side dish for almost everything and I fucking love it. It's one of those things that really shouldn't work but does. It's a very Lithuanian dish and it works well with so many mains.

You could cook the rice the day before and mix it all up at the last minute, but it's far nicer to make it when the rice is still warm. That way, the flavours all meld together beautifully with the warmth from the rice.

Serves 4

Fennel, orange and grape salad

Gaz says

I know I keep saying this, but … this is a banging side dish. It's fruity, it's fresh, it's exactly what you want from a side. There's a bit of creaminess from the mozzarella, a whole lotta zing from the citrus, a bit of sweetness from the grapes and some fragrance from the fennel. It works so well with a fatty, sticky meat that's fresh off the barbecue. The citrus cuts right through that charred crust and it's a match made in heaven.

If I'm barbecuing, I like to choose sides that won't interefere with the cooking on the day. You want everything to be in their bowls, ready to go. Then you're left to focus entirely on the meat, safe in the knowledge that your trusty side dishes are ready for action.

Chef's tip

The fennel needs to be cut as finely as possible. You can cut the fennel using a mandolin set to its second finest setting. But please, for the love of God, be careful. This dressing doesn't need your knuckle blood in it.

Serves 4

1 medium fennel bulb, finely sliced (see the chef's tip)
A good pinch of fine sea salt
125g buffalo mozzarella, torn into chunks
2 oranges, peeled, segmented and pith removed
10 grapes, halved lengthways
2 good handfuls of lamb's lettuce
A pinch of fennel seeds

For the dressing

2 garlic cloves, minced
1 mild fresh red chilli, seeds left in and thinly sliced
6 tablespoons sunflower oil
3 tablespoons white wine vinegar
1 tablespoon fennel seeds
1 teaspoon good-quality smoked paprika
A pinch of chilli flakes

Place all the dressing ingredients into a small pot over a low to medium heat. Warm it gently for 2–3 minutes, swirling the pan often to infuse the flavours.

Meanwhile, put the thinly sliced fennel in a large bowl along with a good seasoning of salt. Pour the dressing over the fennel and toss to coat.

Arrange the fennel on a serving platter and top with the torn chunks of mozzarella, orange segments, grape halves, lamb's lettuce and a scattering of fennel seeds for a bit of pizazz.

Cabbage, garlic and caraway salad

I don't want to give Rita a big head, but this is another one of her concoctions that just knocks it out of the park. It's a really simple dish, but one that sings with flavour.

The key here is to use a nice soft cabbage. You don't want to be chewing each mouthful for half an hour – a good, hearty green cabbage has its place, but it's not right for this dish. A sweetheart cabbage is perfect. It's nice and sweet and will soften down easily in the vinegar and yield to the flavours. Ideally, you'd make this just a few minutes before eating. If the cabbage sits in the dressing for more than 20 minutes, you're at risk of sogginess. And at an Irish barbecue, there's already enough sogginess at play.

Serves 4

2 tablespoons sunflower oil
7 garlic cloves, finely chopped
2 tablespoons caraway seeds
50ml white wine vinegar
50ml very mild sunflower or vegetable oil
1 small head of sweetheart cabbage, finely shredded (around 500g)
3 big pinches of fine sea salt

Heat the 2 tablespoons of sunflower oil in a small saucepan over a low heat. Add the garlic and caraway seeds and warm together for a few minutes. Once that's releasing some lovely aromas, turn the heat off, add the vinegar and the 50ml of the mild sunflower or vegetable oil and stir to combine.

Place the shredded cabbage in a large bowl, coat it with the oil dressing and add three big pinches of salt.

Leave for up to 20 minutes but no longer (see the intro). Give it one last stir just before serving, as the dressing will have snuck its way down to the bottom of the bowl.

Sneaky sauerkraut

Gaz says

We use this all the time at home, but instead of making our own sauerkraut (which takes months), we just buy jars of the stuff and jazz it up a bit. You can find it in all the Polish shops, but if you hit the jackpot you'll find a shop that has it in a wooden barrel, which is how the good stuff is fermented.

Just adding a bit of apple and some caraway seeds makes a world of difference, but don't be tempted to make it too sweet. You want a fairly harsh tang to it — almost too sharp to eat on its own, but perfect when combined with fatty pork or a Polish sausage. Don't base your impression of it on a spoonful from the pan.

Serves 2

30g pancetta or speck, diced
2 tablespoons caraway seeds
1 sweet apple, peeled and thinly sliced or chopped
2 tablespoons caster sugar
300g shop-bought sauerkraut

Heat the speck or pancetta in a saucepan on a low heat until it melts down and releases all that lovely fat. Once it starts to turn golden, turn up the heat to medium so it will crisp up nicely.

Throw in the caraway seeds and heat them up until they have released their aromas. Add the apple and sugar and give it all a good stir to combine. Sweat down the apples and sugar until it's all nicely yielding in the pan. Once it's all softened, add the sauerkraut and heat gently.

Serve with roasted pork or chunks of Polish sausage. It also brings a lot to a sandwich.

A Dublin pub crawl.

Gaz Smith

Rick and I usually do our business deals over a pint in the pub. Neither of us leaves happy! If we can't agree on something, we toss a coin. It's our tradition now – when we go to plan for the following week, we go for a few pints. Funnily enough, our best ideas come after three pints.

We always choose the pubs very carefully. We'd prefer to have no pints of Guinness than a bad Guinness.

When I'm trying to suss out if the Guinness is good, there are a few things I look for. First off, I survey the room like a pint-seeking Terminator. If I see nine auld fellas at the bar, all drinking Guinness with a big shtick on the glass, I'm going straight for that. If no one is drinking Guinness, I'm not going near it.

If I'm unsure, I'll have a chat with the barman and ask him about the draw. One of the key elements to a good Guinness is a short draw – this means that the distance from the keg to the tap is short. If you're in some massive monster pub that keg could be four or five rooms away, which means the line is full of dead Guinness.

In the Sheds, the keg is kept right beneath the tap so there's only two pints in the line. If there are loads of people drinking it, there won't be any in the line. And that makes for a good spanking pint of Guinness.

Nothing beats a perfect pint. It's that first sup … when it's good, it just glides down. I love when the first mouthful of stout pierces the foam and slides into your mouth.

I have WhatsApp groups solely dedicated to pictures of the best pints and where to find them. We can argue all day long about who has the best pint in Dublin. Barry always seems to have the inside scoop about who is pouring the best pint. When his text rolls in, we all descend upon the pub like a swarm of locusts. There are loads of places I love in Dublin, like the Gravediggers in Glasnevin, the Sheds in Clontarf, the Long Hall on George's Street, the Goat in Goatstown Cross and the Swan on Aungier Street. Clarke's in Ringsend and the Raheny Inn are becoming newfound favourites too.

Gaz Smith and Barry Stephens

When I'm trying to suss out if the Guinness is good, there are a few things I look for. First off, I survey the room like a pint-seeking Terminator. If I see nine auld fellas at the bar, all drinking Guinness with a big shtick on the glass, I'm going straight for that. If no one is drinking Guinness, I'm not going near it.

The perfect pub is completely dependent on the barman. They have to know what they're at and they can't be miserable. A grumpy barman puts me off hugely. A good barman knows when to chat to you and when to leave you alone. There are pubs I go to where I only have to glance at the barman and a pint appears in front of me. It's like being at an auction – you cough and they pour you a pint. Once, I sneezed and got a Baileys and Tia Maria.

There have to be loads of little snugs, nooks and crannies. My perfect snug is where very few people can see you, but you have a direct line of sight with the barman. That's where I go when I want to be left alone.

I work weekends, so Tuesday lunchtime is my Saturday night. That's when you'd usually find a few auld fellas with their newspapers. I'd often turn up with some leftovers or nibbles from the restaurants and we'd have a bit of craic. One of my true food pleasures would be a Tuesday lunchtime spent with a carvery plate piled high, a jug of gravy, the papers and a snug. The phone goes away and that's my hour of meditation.

But then there are the days when a Tuesday afternoon turns into a Wednesday morning…

The morning after: Battle of the breakfasts.

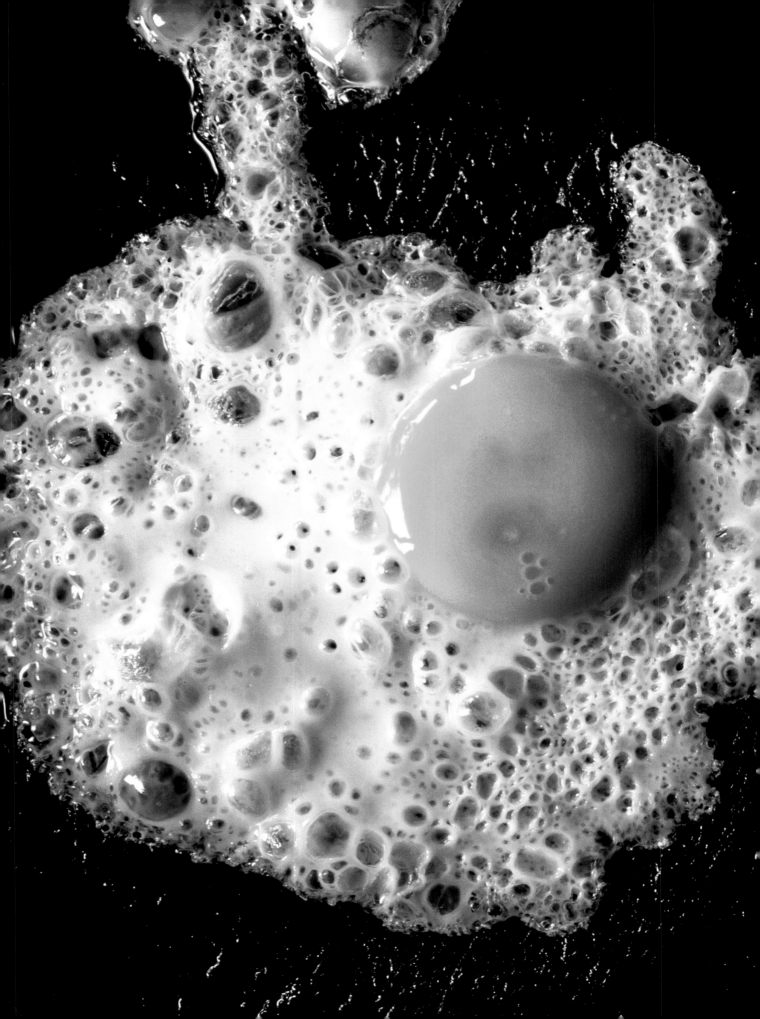

Rick

My perfect fry isn't technically a fry. I never fry the rashers – I always grill them. They have to have the rind on them. If it doesn't have the rind, it's not a real rasher. And none of those paper-thin, see-through rashers. They need to be thick cut.

The sausages have to have a natural skin, not synthetic. I brown them in the frying pan but finish them in the oven, just to make sure they're cooked all the way through. The fry has to have black and white pudding, both done under the grill. Actually, the only thing that has to be fried is the egg. I don't like a crispy egg – I love a sunny side up, medium egg.

You have to have batch toast with a shitload of proper butter on it. I like it when it's melted, but you have to have absolute lashings of butter.

I love beans, but they have to be Batchelors. Have to be! It brings everything together. And they have to be on the plate, not in a fucking ramekin. What kind of tosser would put baked beans in a ramekin?

Gaz

First off, you have to have the baked beans in a ramekin. Only animals let their beans touch their sausage. The beans maketh the fry but I like to be in charge of my own beanage, which is why they always have to be on the side – end of story. I don't want any of their juices touching a single thing on my plate unless I say so.

Now that I've got that off my chest, I can move on to bacon, which has to be thick-cut, unsmoked streaky rashers. When it comes to sausages, I'm actually a fan of skinny sausages. No one's got time to be spending 45 minutes wrapping their chops around a massive sausage. The whole point of a good fry-up is that it all cooks at the same time. Rather than stressing around with a massive, girthy sausage, I want it all to be ready in one fell swoop.

I'd have two frying pans on the go, one nice and low for the hash browns and the eggs, the other one for the sausages and bacon. Wait, there's another pan for the mushrooms. And another for the beans. Okay, okay, so I use a lot of pans, all right? I want my plate to be filled to the brim with everything I can scavenge from the fridge. It needs to be a big plate of bounty or you're not doing it right.

Rita

I only ever like two or three things on my fry. I've got enough on my plate with Gaz. Being from Lithuania, I like some nice speck and eggs. I'd often make what my kids refer to as specky eggs. I pop the lardons of speck and some diced white onion into a dry pan and heat that up until the lardons melt down. When they're almost fully crisp, I crack in two eggs and cook them until they're just barely cooked. I serve that with some delicious Lithuanian rye bread.

I always have that with coffee. A coffee is the only breakfast drink you need.

Hazel Tunney

A coffee is all well and good, but the perfect breakfast beverage is a Slutty Mary. What's a Slutty Mary, you ask? Well, it's a Bloody Mary with a sausage in it. And sometimes a bit of maple-cured bacon too. You pop them both on a skewer and then on top of the glass or on the side. Then you have a sip of cocktail, a bite of sausage, and repeat.

My ideal fry has unsmoked bacon (very few things benefit from being smoked, in my opinion), sausages, fried eggs, something spud-based like scalloped potatoes, black pudding, white pudding and nothing else. Don't forget, you need to put on an extra bit of bacon and sausage for your Slutty Mary.

Most importantly? Nothing touches anything else on the plate. Everything is perfect in and of itself. You can construct every bite from what is on your plate without anything contaminating the other elements. There is no place for beans. At all.

Obviously, you need toasted Brennans white bread with real butter. Preferably almost burnt and left to go a bit cold so it's a little chewy.

Sauces and butters.

Chicken wing gravy 227
New York-style 'gravy' 228
Salsa verde 230
Piquant burger sauce 233
Asian dressing 234
Barry's tzatziki 237
Spiced apple chutney 238
Salted caramel butter 243
Garlic and lemon butter 244
Umami butter 247

Chicken wing gravy

1.2kg chicken wings, bashed up or chopped (see the chef's tip)
1 large onion, quartered
2 carrots, cut into 5cm pieces
2 sprigs of fresh rosemary
1 large bay leaf
3 tablespoons vegetable oil
1 tablespoon fine sea salt
1 tablespoon freshly ground black pepper
100g plain flour
50g butter, diced
2 litres chicken stock (stock cubes or jelly pots are fine)
50ml white wine vinegar
4 sprigs of fresh thyme

Preheat the oven to 200°C.

Arrange the chicken wings, onion, carrots, rosemary and bay leaf on a large baking tray (definitely not a deep-sided roasting tin). Drizzle the whole lot with the oil and season well with the salt and pepper. Toss everything with your hands to make sure all the wings are covered in oil. That way, they'll go nice and crisp and you'll get the maximum amount of flavour in your gravy.

When everything is coated, spread it out in the tray so it's in an even layer. Roast in the oven for about 1 hour, until the wings are golden. If a few are a little burnt looking, that's no harm. Transfer the chicken wings and veg into a large pot.

Add the flour and butter to the hot tray and give it a good old stir until both are well combined and have formed a paste. This is now a basic roux. Steal a cup of the chicken stock to deglaze the tray, then put the whole tray over a low heat on the hob. Gently cook the lot for 4–5 minutes, constantly stirring and scraping up all the brown bits from the bottom of the tray.

Add the white wine vinegar. After 5 minutes, carefully pour all this liquid into the pot with the wings and veg and add the rest of the chicken stock. Give it all a really good stir.

Cook over a low heat for 30–40 minutes. You don't want to let this go to a heavy boil, just a low simmer. Every 10 minutes or so, get a potato masher and give it all a big bash to agitate the flavours from the chicken and the veg. After 30 minutes, give it a taste. You might need to adjust the seasoning, so add a pinch of salt if you do. Add the thyme right at the end.

Once you're happy with the flavour, allow it to sit off the heat for 10 minutes. Strain it through a fine mesh sieve, aggressively squishing out all the chicken wings and veg to get the last of their little flavour bombs out and into the gravy. Try to resist the urge to drink this from a mug, and either pop it in an airtight container in the fridge or freezer or serve with a roast immediately.

Gaz says

I could write a whole book about this gravy. Don't get me wrong – if I'm making a roast at home, more often than not I'll just reach for the Bisto. But once in a while, it's worth taking the time and effort to make a proper gravy. It might seem like a whole load of hassle, but it really isn't. This is one to make on a rainy Sunday afternoon when you've got nothing better to be doing.

If you're cooking a roast, all the pressure is off once you've got a good gravy already made. You can make a hash of most of the dinner, but if you're slathering the whole lot in a gorgeous, glossy, flavour-packed gravy, nothing else matters.

This one freezes really well, so you can always have a batch of it to hand. If I'm roasting a chicken, I'll often just make this gravy at the same time – the oven is already on, so whacking a tray of wings in at the same time is no bother.

Chef's tip

If you're getting your chicken wings from the butcher, get them to hammer up the wings for you when they're raw. All the flavour is inside the bones and gristle, so you'll get a far tastier gravy out of it. If not, snip them up at home as best you can, even just to break the skin.

New York-style 'gravy'

Gaz says

Look, we all know that I love gravy. But put away the thoughts of the gravy that we know and love, because New York-style 'gravy' is actually a rich tomato sauce. Technically it's an Italian-American sauce beloved by New Yorkers, but now we're just making things complicated.

In this one, you get all the flavours of the rich Italian sausage and the pork, cooked down for hours over a low heat. It's not a ragù and it's not a Bolognese, but it's somewhere in the same family.

This goes incredibly well with the lamb neck meatballs (page 112) and is excellent with pasta too. It's also a handy one to keep portions of as you can chuck it in loads of dishes. This recipe makes a lot (but even so, there's also no harm in going ahead and doubling the recipe), so freeze it in ice cube trays, then pop the frozen cubes into a freezerproof ziplock bag to use in the oysters with a Bloody Mary sauce (page 23), smoked haddock and prawn lasagne (page 50) and the beef tartare (page 86).

2 tablespoons vegetable oil
2 medium onions, roughly chopped
8 garlic cloves, roughly chopped
1 teaspoon chilli flakes (optional)
500ml red wine (plus a bit for the chef)
2 x 400g tins of chopped tomatoes
120g good-quality tomato purée (I like Mutti)
500ml beef stock
A pinch of dried oregano
5 big pinches of fine sea salt
5 big pinches of freshly ground black pepper
300g Italian sausage, left whole
200g pork ribs
A big pinch of fresh basil leaves, torn

Put your biggest pot on a low to medium heat. Add your vegetable oil, then add the onions and garlic and sweat for 8–10 minutes. Add your chilli flakes here too if you're using them.

Pour in your red wine and bring it to the boil. Drink 250ml of red wine yourself because ... well, you opened the bottle, didn't you? You don't want to let it go to waste. Reduce the wine in the pan by half, which should take 5–6 minutes.

Add the chopped tomatoes, tomato purée, beef stock, oregano and salt and pepper. Chuck in your whole sausages and pork ribs. Turn down the heat, cover the pot and simmer the whole lot very gently for 60 minutes, then remove the lid and simmer for 30 minutes more. Smile as your house fills with the scent of warm, sausagey, tomatoey goodness.

When you think it's done, check the seasoning, then fish out the whole sausages and pork ribs. Finish it off with a big pinch of torn basil leaves.

Salsa verde

Gaz says

This is one of my classic go-to sauces. It's zingy, sharp and packed with flavour. It's brilliant drizzled over a roasted chicken, a leg of lamb or some fresh fish. But it's equally good thrown in a sandwich or with some leftover meat cold out of the fridge.

I sometimes add an extra dash of white wine vinegar just before using, but I'm a whore for really sharp dressings. If you're the same, give it a go, particularly if it's been sitting in the fridge for a few days.

It might seem a little strong when you taste it, but when it's drizzled over something, all the flavours will balance themselves out.

100g fresh basil leaves
25g fresh flat-leaf parsley
20g fresh tarragon leaves
6 garlic cloves, minced
150ml vegetable oil
80ml extra virgin olive oil
4 tablespoons white wine vinegar
4 tablespoons wholegrain mustard
3 tablespoons Dijon mustard
2 tablespoons Colman's mint sauce
2 teaspoons fine sea salt

Place all the ingredients in the bowl of a food processor and whizz to form a thick, smooth consistency. This will keep in an airtight container in the fridge for a good few days.

Piquant burger sauce

200ml mayonnaise
50ml ketchup
50ml yellow American mustard
12 slices of sweet pickles or gherkins (not cornichons)
100ml of the brine from your jar of pickles
2 tablespoons Worcestershire sauce
2 teaspoons sweet paprika
2 teaspoons cayenne pepper
1 teaspoon garlic powder
A good pinch of fine sea salt

Blitz it all up in a food processor or blender until it's well combined and very piquant.

Keep it in the fridge and slather it thickly on a burger bun when you're making burgers (like the smash burgers on page 176).

Asian dressing

Gaz says

This sauce is king of the kitchen. Once you've got a batch of this made up, you can use it on pretty much anything. It's the basis of our amazing tuna tartare (page 52), it's the key to the Asian noodle salad (page 195) and we even chuck it into the dirty 'fried' rice (page 167). Basically, it's always a good idea to have a batch of this ready to go in the fridge. Try it once and you'll never be without it again.

4 garlic cloves, crushed
1 spring onion, thinly sliced
1 medium-hot fresh long red chilli, very finely chopped
A pinch of chilli flakes
A small handful of fresh coriander, finely chopped
1 x 25g piece of fresh ginger, peeled and grated
20g white sesame seeds
280ml soy sauce (we use regular Kikkoman soy sauce)
100ml white wine vinegar
100ml sweet chilli sauce
40ml toasted sesame oil
50ml mirin
40ml fish sauce
2 tablespoons XO sauce
1 tablespoon Maggi Liquid Seasoning

Add all the ingredients into a mixing bowl and whisk to combine. This will store in an airtight container in the fridge for two weeks.

Barry's tzatziki

Barry says

I love tzatziki with any kind of grilled meat, but it goes particularly well with charred lamb straight off the barbecue. In my eyes, it's the perfect combination – charred, smoky, sticky meat and a zingy, fresh tzatziki.

The key to preventing your tzatziki from splitting is salting the grated cucumber and leaving it for at least an hour. Just leave it in the strainer and forget about it. Then, when you're ready to use it, squeeze the excess liquid out of it by hand. The longer you leave it, the more moisture you'll get out of the cucumber.

1 big cucumber, grated
200g Greek yoghurt
1 garlic clove, crushed
2 tablespoons good-quality olive oil
1 tablespoon finely chopped fresh mint
1 tablespoon lemon juice
½ tablespoon finely chopped fresh dill
½ teaspoon toasted sesame seeds
Fine sea salt and freshly ground black pepper

Put your grated cucumber into a sieve and cover it in salt. Leave it in the kitchen sink for at least 1 hour. After an hour, give it a good squeeze to get as much water out of it as you can. A clean tea towel does the trick nicely. Give it a bit of muscle!

Add all the other ingredients into a food processer and whizz to combine.

Fold the grated cucumber through the yoghurt mix and season to taste.

Spiced apple chutney

It's always good to have a bit of this knocking around the fridge. It's a key ingredient in the black pudding strudel (page 185) but it's just as good in a sambo or with a few big slabs of cheese of an evening. You can always double the recipe and keep a batch of it to hand.

1 tablespoon sunflower oil
½ medium brown onion, roughly chopped
300g dates, pitted
190g light brown sugar
4 large cooking apples, peeled and quartered (around 1kg)
120ml white wine vinegar
100ml apple juice
Juice of 2 oranges
3 star anise
3 tablespoons ground cinnamon
3 tablespoons allspice
3 tablespoons fine sea salt
3 tablespoons water

Warm the oil in a saucepan over a medium heat, then add the onion and sauté for 3–4 minutes, stirring often, until it's softened. Add all the other ingredients and combine well.

Cover with a lid and turn the heat down to a low to medium heat, cooking until the apples have softened. This should take about 15 minutes. Remove the lid, turn the heat down to its lowest setting and continue to cook very gently for another 20 minutes, stirring occasionally to make sure it doesn't stick to the bottom of the pan.

If you prefer your chutney a little thicker, gently simmer it without a lid to reduce it down a little. Just keep a close eye on it so it doesn't catch at the bottom and burn.

This will keep in an airtight container in the fridge for a week or so.

Gaz says
This might be a bit of shocking statement, but bear with me:

I love butter.

We always have three different butters on the go in Michael's – one lemon, one lemon and garlic, and one just garlic. We use different ratios depending on the dish, but almost everything we cook is finished with a spoonful of butter in the pan. In my eyes, that's all you need. When you have a piece of spanking fresh fish, it doesn't need a load of wankery on the side. One of my pet hates is seeing fish on a menu with five or six things around it that you simply don't need. The fish needs to be the star of the show. And the butter is the supporting star that makes it all just that little bit better.

Here are three of my favourites.

Salted caramel butter

1 x 454g block of butter, softened
20g toasted hazelnuts, finely chopped
A good pinch of fine sea salt

For the butterscotch
100g caster sugar
A splash of lemon juice
40g butter
50ml pouring or fresh cream

To make the butterscotch, melt the sugar and a few drops of lemon juice in a small saucepan over a low heat, swirling the pan occasionally until it's a nice bronze colour. This should take around 15 minutes, but don't try to rush this process or you'll burn the sugar. It's important that you only swirl the pan, not stir it, otherwise lumps could form in your caramel. And don't be tempted to lick the spoon, molten sugar is no joke.

The moment the sugar turns bronze, take the pan off the heat, add the 40g of butter and stir well to combine. Pour in the cream and again stir the whole lot to combine. Remove the pan from the heat and leave it to cool to room temperature.

When you're ready to mix the two, whip your 454g block of butter in a stand mixer with the spade attachment on a medium speed until it's super soft and smooth. We whip this for bloody ages in the restaurant – basically, you want to get it as light and fluffy as you can. When you've got it nice and smooth, add the nuts and salt.

Turn up the speed on the mixer and pour in your butterscotch in a slow, steady, delicious stream. Carry on whipping for at least 5 or 6 minutes, it until it's ever so slightly bigger in the bowl and nice and creamy.

Once it's finished, you can get really jazzy and roll it up in cling film into the shape of a giant sausage and keep it in the fridge, ready to slice off when you need it. If you do, be sure to burst any air bubbles that form along the way. But if that's too much effort, just whack it in a bowl or an airtight container.

Slather this on warm bread, hot popcorn or anything else that takes your fancy. Wink wink.

Gaz says
This might sound like a strange one, but we wanted something a little different to serve with warm bread in the restaurant. And this butter hits the nail on the head – it's that gorgeous mix of sweet and salty that adds something special to the plate. I didn't think it would be as popular as it is, but people just love it. We even sold it by the tub during the first lockdown in 2020.

Like most of my stupid little ideas, there wasn't much of a thought process behind it. But it just works. Basically, you're making a butterscotch sauce, then blending that in whipped butter. What you're left with is a gorgeous, soft, sweet and salty butter. Whack it on warm bread, let it drip down your chin and all your cares will just drift away.

Garlic and lemon butter

Gaz says

This is very simple, but we get through an absolute ton of it in the restaurants. And with good reason. Everything is better once you've got this butter on the plate, whether it's a thick hunk of lobster or a pile of golden chips.

We use the juice and zest of a lemon (so you get all those fragrant oils), fresh garlic and the best salted butter. Unsalted butter has no place on this planet. Our handy little trick? Whipping the butter, which makes it brown and foam better in the pan.

Once it's done, you can keep it in the fridge for an age, then use it however your perverted little heart desires. Just send me pictures afterwards.

1 x 454g block of butter, softened
3 large garlic cloves, very finely chopped or grated
Zest and juice of 1 big lemon

Get your butter nice and soft.

Um … mix all together.

That's it.

Umami butter

Gaz says

To me, umami is the essence of deliciousness. Things like fish sauce, dried ceps, anchovies, Marmite … they all have that distinct smack of umami that sticks with you long after you've licked the plate clean. This butter wraps up all those heavenly umami flavours and ties them in a little bow.

There's nothing weak about this butter. If you were to whack this on a steak, the steak and this butter would do battle to the end, like some kind of Batman vs. Superman, both of whom you want to lick. You could also cook some mushrooms in a whole load of this butter, slather the lot on a thick slab of toast and you'd pretty much die of happiness.

250g butter
50g porcini or cep powder
4 garlic cloves, very finely minced or grated
25ml red wine vinegar
2 teaspoons Worcestershire sauce
2 teaspoons fish sauce
1 teaspoon Maggi Liquid Seasoning

Get the butter slightly warmed, but not melted. With a wooden spoon, beat in all the other ingredients. Pop it in a container and either use it straight away or stash it in the fridge.

Desserts.

Date, maple and macadamia cake   252
Chocolate Amarena cherry brownie cake   254
Hand-selected assiette of petit fours   257

Date, maple and macadamia cake

Gaz says

When I sit down in a restaurant I always pretend to the waiter that I'm not going to have a dessert, which is why I can order two starters instead. Then, when it's time for dessert, I just hope that he's graceful enough to pretend that our earlier conversation didn't happen. Because I'm damn well getting a dessert. And then a cheese course. Maybe another main too.

This is my idea of a perfect dessert. It's basically a sticky toffee pudding with some macadamia nuts thrown in the mix. There's no cheffy wankery to – we're not trying to break the mould here. It's just about using ingredients that work really fucking well together.

This is amazing served warm with ice cream or even cold as a cake with an afternoon coffee. If it survives that long, that is.

Serves 8

100g macadamia nuts
1 vanilla pod, cut in half lengthways
225g whole Medjool dates, pitted
175ml boiling water
175g self-raising flour, plus extra for dusting
1 teaspoon baking powder
85g butter, softened, plus extra for greasing
140g demerara sugar
2 tablespoons black treacle
2 eggs, beaten
100ml milk
120ml maple syrup
1 teaspoon caster sugar

To serve
Whipped cream or ice cream

Toast the macadamia nuts in a dry frying pan over a medium heat until they're lightly golden. Scatter them on a clean tea towel with the sides bunched over or decant into a large ziplock bag and bash them all up with a rolling pin.

Scrape the seeds from inside the vanilla pod and set aside.

Put the dates, boiling water and scraped-out vanilla pod into a medium saucepan. Wrap the top of the saucepan with cling film and cover with a lid to create a very tight seal, being careful that the cling film won't melt over a direct heat. It's key not to let the water evaporate – the tighter the seal, the nicer your cake will be. If too much water escapes, your cake will end up dry and crappy. Gently simmer for 15–20 minutes, then set aside for 20 minutes to cool.

Preheat the oven to 180°C. Grease and line a 23cm springform cake tin with non-stick baking paper.

Sift the flour and baking powder into a big mixing bowl.

Cream the butter and demerara sugar together in a stand mixer on a medium speed for 4–5 minutes, until it's light and fluffy.

Remove the vanilla pod from the dates and discard. Add the treacle to the dates and blitz with a stick blender for 30 seconds, until you're left with a thick paste.

Add one-third of the beaten eggs and all the vanilla seeds into the butter and sugar mixture, followed by one-third of the milk and one-third of the flour. Beat well, then repeat the egg–milk–flour process twice more, using a third of the ingredients each time, scraping down the sides of the bowl with a spatula. Add the dates and combine until you're left with a coarse, somewhat lumpy batter.

Scatter the toasted macadamia nuts over the base of your lined tin, drizzle with half the maple syrup and sprinkle with the teaspoon of sugar. Spoon the batter over the nuts and spread it out evenly.

Bake in the oven for 25–30 minutes, until the cake is golden brown on top and a little jiggly to touch in the middle. You want it to be ever so slightly gooey inside. Poke a few holes in the cake and drizzle with the remaining maple syrup.

Allow the cake to cool slightly before removing from the tin and cutting into slices. Serve with whipped cream or ice cream.

Chocolate Amarena cherry brownie cake

Gaz says

Look, I'm not going to claim that I've invented the chocolate brownie. But this is a fairly typical dessert that everyone should have in their back pocket. It's a staple.

What sets this one apart is the cherries. Oh, the cherries. It can be a little more work to source them, but it's fairly easy to find Amarena cherries nowadays. You can even get them in Lidl every so often. Don't even bother making this with fresh, frozen or glacé cherries because it won't be the same. Like the macadamia nuts in the cake on page 252, it's the cherries that make this dish.

Serves 6

75g plain flour
50g cocoa powder
4 large free-range eggs
300g caster sugar
200g butter, melted, plus extra for greasing
100g plain dark chocolate (70% cocoa solids), chopped into chunks
200g Amarena cherries in syrup, plus extra to serve

To serve
Whipped cream or vanilla ice cream

Preheat the oven to 180°C. Grease and line a 23cm springform cake tin with non-stick baking paper.

Sift the flour and cocoa twice, then combine in a large bowl and set aside.

Lightly whisk the eggs in a stand mixer on a low to medium speed. Add the sugar, melted butter and chopped chocolate, then gently fold in the cherries using a spatula. Gently fold in the flour and cocoa powder, making sure you scrape up everything from the bottom of the bowl with the spatula.

Turn the batter out into the prepared tin and bake in the oven for 45–50 minutes. After 40 minutes, poke the cake with a skewer and see how it's getting on – you want it to still be a little moist inside.

When it's ready, remove from the oven and allow to cool for a few minutes before poking a few holes in the cake with a skewer and drizzling 4–5 tablespoons of the Amarena cherry syrup from the jar all over the top of the cake.

Serve topped with a few more of the cherries along with whipped cream or vanilla ice cream.

Hand-selected assiette of petit fours

Gaz says

There's a lot of thought that goes into making a really good dessert. This is the kind of cooking that requires careful precision. You need sugar thermometers, professional-grade mixers, infinite patience and a delicate hand. This recipe might seem like a lot of work, but I promise you, it's worth it in the end.

Serves 1

1 bag of Jelly Snakes
1 big bag of Galaxy Minstrels
1 big bag of Haribo Giant Strawberries

Place your Jelly Snakes in your fanciest bowl. These are best eaten off bone china or cut crystal – the natural sugars in the snakes require an even-temperature surface that only the finest materials can provide.

Open the bag of Minstrels ever so gently and place them in and around the Jelly Snakes. You're not just 'dumping a load of sweets in a bowl', let me tell you that for nothing.

Finally, open the bag of Giant Strawberries and delicately intersperse them between the Jelly Snakes and the Minstrels.

Eat with a mother of pearl caviar spoon.

Substitutions

If you cannot source Minstrels in your local gourmet grocery store, you may substitute Maltesers.

If Giant Strawberries are not in season, you may swap these out for Haribo Starmix.

If Jelly Snakes are not available, abandon the recipe entirely. This carefully deduced concoction relies specifically on Jelly Snakes and any other substitution would throw off the balance of the entire dish.

The Higgins' crew.

I spent 16 years working for and with my parents, Tony and Rose. When the opportunity arose to bring the family business back to Sutton Cross, the only people who believed that I could make a go of it were my parents. They encouraged me when everyone else thought I was mad. Even though my dad is fully retired, he will always be an integral part of the team. He's still the master to me – I often bounce ideas off him and ask his advice. He'll be the first to tell me if I'm doing something wrong or right. His opinion is so important to me and to the continued success of Higgins Butchers. I idolise both of my parents and owe them so much.

The team we have in Sutton is second to none, a gang of hardened old-school butchers who aren't afraid to take on modern techniques and put up with my crazy ideas and aspirations. I'm blessed to have their 100% support no matter what and I always have their backs too.

It's a two-way street, though – I give them the freedom to express themselves when they come up with something new or something that I haven't thought of before. We have great banter and I would like to think that I'm not just a boss, but also a mate and someone who's on a level with them.

They're all legends and I couldn't do it without them.

Rick Higgins

Jean Higgins

Jean is the rock who keeps us all grounded. She's my sister and we have a great relationship – she's also not afraid to tell me to fuck off from time to time. She's a grafter and there's nothing I wouldn't do for her. She's like my work mammy.

John Ramsay

John is a proper old-school butcher who would put most butchers to shame with a knife in his hand. He's the quick-witted one who has his head down all day and only lifts it to drop in a one-liner. He's great craic and awesome with the customers. His knowledge and level head bring a sense of calm to the team.

Shane McFadden

Shane is my workhorse and I would trust him with my life. He started his training under my dad's wing and when my dad retired, I snapped him up. He's only in his early thirties but he's already a legend and a world-class butcher. He has a great sense of humour and the customers adore him. Shane would do anything for me and that works both ways.

Jules Mahon

Jules is a big ray of sunshine, but more than that, she's a really solid sounding board, always calm, always measured and always ready with solid advice that guides me greatly on a day-to-day basis. She's a brilliant asset. Since coming on board as executive wine director she's put together lists that rival any others and she does it with a smile. She also knows the filthiest jokes.

The Michael's crew.

I get called Michael 50 times a day. To be honest, it makes sense – after all, I do own a restaurant called Michael's. When we somehow managed to take it over from the original owner, Michael Lowe, we didn't have two pennies to rub together. We were completely broke, but loads of work had to be done and we had to make some tough choices. For example, we had to decide between buying the freshest seafood we could find or paying to change the name. And of course, we chose the seafood. We believed that if the seafood was fresh enough, people would sit on milk crates to enjoy it. The name over the door didn't matter.

The real success story behind the restaurant is the team. We're lucky that we've had the same people working here for years – one or two of them have even worked in Michael's longer than I have! The core management team of Luiza, Hannah, Caoimhe, Clare, Djeny, Jules, Emma and Keith are the reckoning force behind the whole operation. But we're so lucky – everyone on the team is incredible.

Our typical day is the perfect combination of us being super professional, then incredibly unprofessional. There's always messing, constant pranks and belly laughs. But that's what helps us to break up the long working days.

Gaz Smith

Nenad Platisa

We call him Neno, but his full name is Nenad. He's my right-hand man in the restaurant and he cooks like an absolute machine. Neno would be your warhorse in a busy service and he takes great pride in what he does. He detests fish sauce, so one of our pranks would be to put a dab of it in his bike helmet.

Ivan Šepčić

Ivan is the head chef in Little Mike's and provides great support for Neno as well. They've been best friends since school – they work as a unit. Ivan is a creative and caring chef who's always in work half an hour early and there for half an hour after his shift ends too. Even better, he's always good for a nice long boozy staff lunch of a Monday when we're all off work.

Keith Hallissey

Keith is a stalwart of the Dublin restaurant trade and he's adored by anyone who meets him. He's treated Little Mike's like his own baby since the first day. He watches the cutlery and glasses like a hawk, counting them at the start and end of every shift. Obviously, we get our giggles from hiding them from him or pretending a Zalto has been smashed. But when I actually do break a glass, I'm terrified of a stern telling-off from Keith. I get scolded like a schoolboy.

Clare Scally

Clare is from Rathmullan and is obsessed with bingo. At every single staff party, she forces us all to play. She's the assistant manager at Michael's and whenever she needs cheering up, we play Daniel O'Donnell's 'Jambalaya' – she could be halfway through serving a table and would cry 'G'wan, ya boya!' as soon as she hears it.

Index

apple chutney 238
Asian dressing 234
Asian noodle salad 195
Asian-style slaw 192
Asian-style tuna tartare 52
assiette of petit fours 257
avocado purée 37

Barry's Asian-style slaw 192
Barry's Dublin dip 179
Barry's Indian-spiced monkfish 58
Barry's tzatziki 237
béchamel sauce 50
beef
    beef tartare, Austrian style 86
    bone marrow with mushroom vinaigrette 94
    fillet on the bone 132
    flanken-cut beef ribs 97
    hanger steak 134
    how to cook a steak 129
    how to prepare a prime rib of beef 118–119
    picanha steak 130
    reverse-seared rib of beef 136–137
    smash burger 176
    temperature cooking guidelines 129
Behan, Derek 71, 75
black pudding strudel 185
black sole on the bone with capers and gherkins 56
Bloody Mary sauce 23
bone marrow with mushroom vinaigrette 94
Brady, Nicola 61–74, 141–154
breaded lamb chops with zappy buttermilk dressing 85
breakfasts, battle of 216–221
burger
    piquant burger sauce 233
    smash burger 176
butchery masterclass 115–123
buttermilk dressing 85
butters
    garlic and lemon butter 244
    salted caramel butter 243
    umami butter 247

cabbage, garlic and caraway salad 201
chicken
    chicken hearts in Jägermeister sauce 93
    chicken thighs in soy and mirin marinade 91
    chicken, turnip and barley stew 162
    chicken wing gravy 227
    how to spatchcock a chicken 122–123
    one-hour roast chicken 161
chocolate Amarena cherry brownie cake 254
cockles
    cockle linguine 40
    seafood chowder 47
crab
    crab claws in garlic and lemon butter 30
    crab omelette 39
    crab salad with avocado purée and pickled cucumber 37

crisp sandwich 173
curry, jungle curry 164

date, maple and macadamia cake 252
desserts
    assiette of petit fours 257
    chocolate Amarena cherry brownie cake 254
    date, maple and macadamia cake 252
dirty 'fried' rice with sesame, chilli and ginger 167
dressings
    Asian dressing 234
    buttermilk dressing 85
    hazelnut and tarragon vinaigrette 24
    mushroom vinaigrette 94
Dublin Bay prawns 34
Dublin crab 61–75
Dublin dip, Barry's 179
Dublin pub crawl 205–215

Farren, Steven 2, 66, 67, 68
fennel, orange and grape salad 198
fillet on the bone 132
fish and chips with pea purée 48
flanken-cut beef ribs 97
Flynn, Maria 2
fried Gruyère and honey sandwich 174

garlic and lemon butter 244

haddock, smoked haddock and prawn lasagne 50
hake and mussels in garlic and lemon butter 55
Hallissey, Keith 264
hand-selected assiette of petit fours 257
hanger steak 134
Higgins, Eva 9, 10
Higgins, Jean 260
Higgins, Rose 9, 259
Higgins, Tony 9, 260

jungle curry (that isn't) 164

lamb
    Barry's lamb shoulder with mother sauce 82
    breaded lamb chops with zappy buttermilk dressing 85
    how to French trim a rack of lamb 116–117
    lamb neck meatballs with New York-style 'gravy' 112
    lamb shanks with dill, turmeric and chilli 81
Lowe, Michael 263

Maggi Liquid Seasoning 17
Markey, Ger 2, 60, 62, 66, 67, 68, 70, 71, 74
Markey, Rob 2, 60, 62, 66, 67, 71, 74
McFadden, Shane 260
meatballs, lamb neck meatballs with a New York-style 'gravy' 112
monkfish, Barry's Indian-spiced monkfish 58
Mooney, John 60, 65, 67, 71, 74
mother sauce 82
mushroom and mozzarella arancini 186–189
mussels
    hake and mussels in garlic and lemon butter 55
    in a coconut, chilli and coriander seed broth 27
    seafood chowder 47

Nenad's venison goulash 111
New York-style 'gravy' 228

O'Gorman Meats 140–155
O'Gorman, James 142, 143, 145
O'Gorman, Jim 143
O'Gorman, Niall 142, 143, 144, 146, 147, 154
one-hour roast chicken 161
one-pot wonders
    chicken, turnip and barley stew 162
    dirty 'fried' rice with sesame, chilli and ginger 167
    jungle curry (that isn't) 164
    one-hour roast chicken 161
oysters
    with a Bloody Mary sauce 23
    with a hazelnut and tarragon vinaigrette 24

pea purée 48
pheasant shepherd's pie 98
picanha steak 130
piquant burger sauce 233
Platisa, Nenad 111, 264
porchetta
    Barry's porchetta 102
    how to stuff and roll a porchetta 120–121
pork
    Barry's porchetta 102
    how to stuff and roll a porchetta 120–121
    jungle curry 164
    pork porterhouse with salsa verde 88
    pork stelze 104
    roast pork belly with cumin and lime 106–107
potatoes, 60:40 mash 191
prawns
    Dublin Bay prawns 34
    grilled prawns in a caramel and fish sauce glaze 32
    seafood chowder 47
    smoked haddock and prawn lasagne 50

Ramsay, John 260
rib of beef, reverse-seared 136–137
rice
    dirty 'fried' rice with sesame, chilli and ginger 167
    Rita's rice salad 197
roast pork belly with cumin and lime 106-107

salads
    Asian noodle salad 195
    Barry's Asian-style slaw 192
    cabbage, garlic and caraway salad 201
    fennel, orange and grape salad 198
    Rita's rice salad 197
salsa verde 230
salted caramel butter 243
sandwiches
    Barry's Dublin dip 179
    crisp sandwich 173
    fried Gruyère and honey sandwich 174
sauces
    Asian dressing 234

Barry's tzatziki 237
    béchamel 50
    Bloody Mary sauce 23
    chicken wing gravy 227
    mother sauce 82
    New York-style 'gravy' 228
    piquant burger sauce 233
    salsa verde 230
    spiced apple chutney 238
sauerkraut, sneaky sauerkraut 203
scallops, seared with cucumber and mint gazpacho 29
Scally, Clare 264
seafood
    Asian-style tuna tartare 52
    Barry's Indian-spiced monkfish 58
    black sole on the bone with capers and gherkins 56
    chowder 47
    fish and chips with pea purée 48
    hake and mussels in garlic and lemon butter 55
    smoked haddock and prawn lasagne 50
Šepčić, Ivan 264
shellfish
    cockle linguine 40
    crab claws in garlic and lemon butter 30
    crab omelette 39
    crab salad with avocado purée and pickled cucumber 37
    Dublin Bay prawns 34
    grilled prawns in a caramel and fish sauce glaze 32
    hake and mussels in garlic and lemon butter 55
    mussels in a coconut, chilli and coriander seed broth 27
    oysters with a Bloody Mary sauce 23
    oysters with a hazelnut and tarragon vinaigrette 24
    seared scallops with cucumber and mint gazpacho 29
    smoked haddock and prawn lasagne 50
sides
    60:40 mash 191
    black pudding strudel 185
    mushroom and mozzarella arancini 186–189
    sneaky sauerkraut 203
smash burger 176
Smith, Rita 2, 10, 27, 71, 161, 197, 201, 219
smoked haddock and prawn lasagne 50
sneaky sauerkraut 203
spiced apple chutney 238
steaks
    fillet on the bone 132
    hanger 134
    how to cook 129
    picanha 130
    reverse-seared rib of beef 136–137
Stephens, Barry 15, 58, 82, 102, 179, 192, 206, 210, 211, 212, 237

tuna, Asian-style tuna tartare 52
Tunney, Hazel 219
tzatziki 237

umami butter 247

venison, Nenad's venison goulash 111

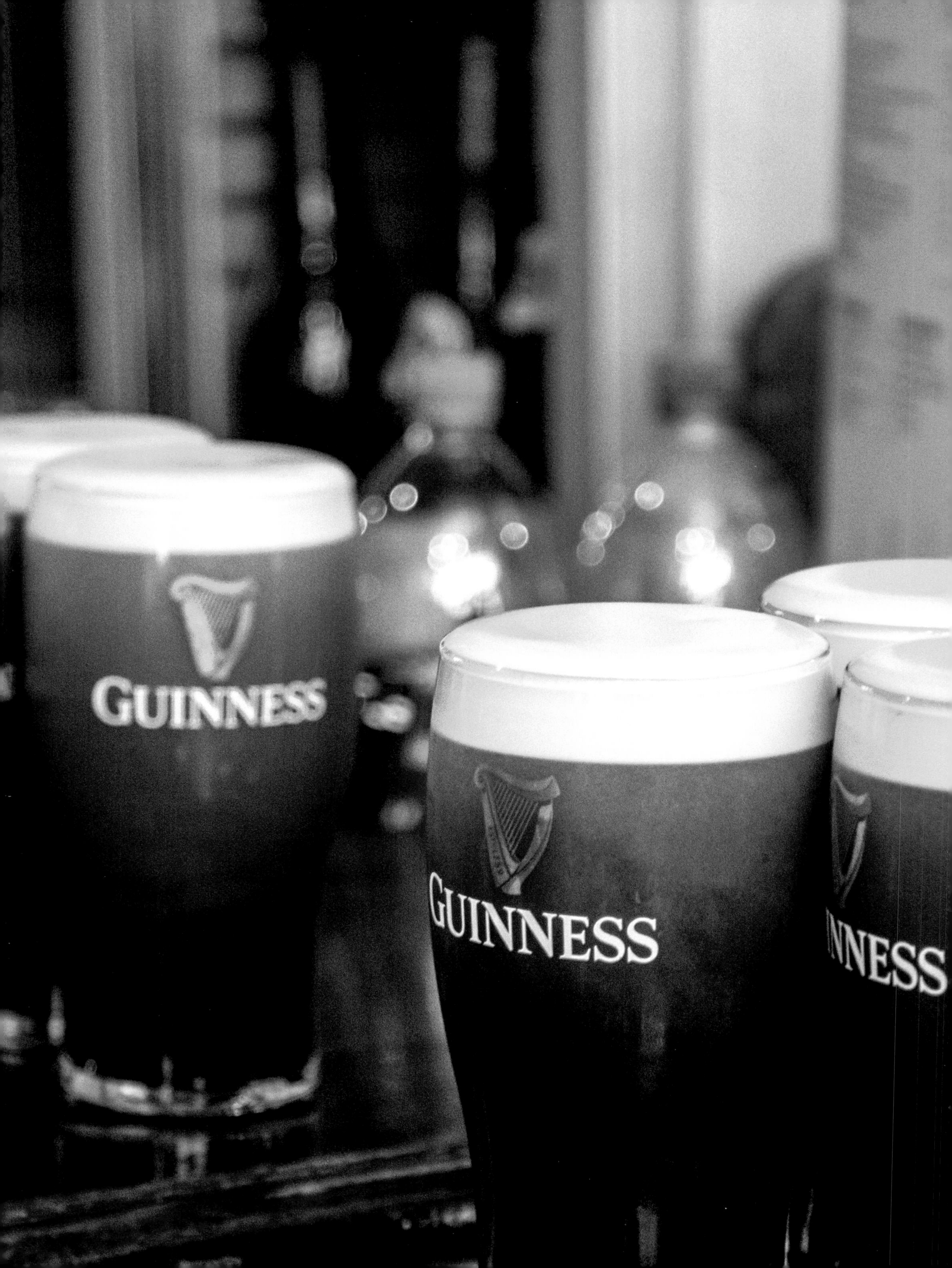
GUINNESS
GUINNESS

Cheers!

We bounced different aspects of this book off of many people who have all been extremely generous with their time and knowledge. I'm reluctant to write this page because you always forget a name, so if you did help and I missed you out, don't take it personally – you know I'm a fecking eejit.

I want to thank every single one of the team at Michael's who have covered me and helped to make this happen. In the kitchen in particular, Craig, Ivan, Djeni and Joao helped with the recipe testing and the carnage that ensued. You can only imagine how that kitchen looked when we were finished.

Then, of course, I want to thank Nicola, Katie, John, Kristin and Barry. Like everything we do, we did this book arseways. We went to a publisher right at the very end instead of at the start, and if we'd known how hard it would be to do in such a short timeframe, I don't think we would have done it. But they all bent over backwards and beavered away. I'm very proud of what they accomplished – this really shouldn't have worked! We shouldn't be sat here after making a book in three months. But we have. So thank you.

I also want to thank Hazel Tunney, who has been a great sounding board throughout, well, pretty much everything, and Hannah Douglas, who's like my consigliere and keeps me in line. Hannah gets me firmly in the zone early every Monday morning, though I know I'm in trouble when she starts the conversation with 'Gareth', not Gaz.

We also want to thank James and Niall O'Gorman as well as Steven Farren, John Mooney, and Ger and Rob Markey.

Rick and I want to thank our wives, Rita and Eva, for putting up with this project on top of our usual nonsense.

Rick would also like to thank all the team in the shop: Shane, John, Ray, Darren and of course his sister, Jean.

And of course, we want to thank all our amazing customers from Michael's, Little Mike's and Higgins Family Butcher.

I want to thank my mum, Margo, who despite my penchant for missing school always kept at me to write stories and encouraged me to write a book from a young age. I wish she'd got to read it. Sleep easy.

Finally, we want to thank all our Twitter followers, who have always been so full of encouragement. They spurred us on to finally do this – so really, it's all their fault!

Gaz Smith

Nine Bean Rows Books Ltd
23 Mountjoy Square
Dublin 1
Ireland
ninebeanrowsbooks.com

First published 2021

ISBN: 978-1-7399858-0-6

Writer: Nicola Brady
Art director, food stylist, food photographer and photo editing: Katie Quinn
Props: Anne Marie Tobin
Lifestyle photographer: John Murray (pages vi, 3, 6–7, 8, 11, 12–13, 60, 63, 65, 69, 70, 72–73, 75, 114, 116–123, 128, 138–139, 144–145, 148–149, 151, 152, 153, 155, 204, 207, 208–209, 210, 211, 212, 214–215, 258, 261, 262, 265, 266–267, 270)
Design and layout: Katie Quinn
Editor: Kristin Jensen
Indexer: Kate Murphy
Printed by Colorman Ireland

A CIP catalogue record for this book is available from the British Library.

10 9 8 7 6 5 4 3 2 1